CULTURAL POLITICS OF MODERN INDIA

CULTURAL POLITICS OF MODERN INDIA

Ajay Gudavarthy

CULTURAL POLITICS OF MODERN INDIA
Ajay Gudavarthy

First Published 2015

ISBN 978-93-5002-383-9 (Hb)

Published by
AAKAR BOOKS
28 E Pocket IV, Mayur Vihar Phase I, Delhi 110 091
Phone : 011 2279 5505 Telefax : 011 2279 5641
aakarbooks@gmail.com; www.aakarbooks.com

Printed at
Sapra Brothers, Delhi 110 092

Dedicated to

Gurpreet Mahajan

Friend, Philosopher, Guide

Contents

THE MODI PHENOMENON

LEFT IN INDIA

DALIT POLITICS AND RESERVATIONS

STATE AND DEMOCRACY

THE CITIZENSHIP DEBATE

Introduction

This book is a collection of short essays written for various news dailies, magazines and journals, primarily focusing on current political developments in India, for the last decade or so. They however draw from the cultural resources of the place, in order to understand how political discourses are getting framed. 'Cultural Politics' is essentially about meaning-making of the political process bringing into relief the significance of symbols, representation, values, and social mores. The attempt is to understand the interface between culture, politics and economic changes, what E.P.Thompson refers to as 'moral economy' of contested meanings. Alongside the attempt is also to understand policy, institutions, and political processes in their intricate details, and everyday functioning. These are essentially synoptic 'first take' on the issues discussed here. Put together, they attempt to give an initial frame to the fast changing essence of politics and culture in India.

In India cultural identities include the relations of power and politics of domination and subordination around caste, class, gender, ethnicity/race, language, religion, history and memory, among other factors. The process becomes all the more complex with the interface between all of them at times, and assertion of some over others by way of supplanting and subsuming, at others. At what point do these factors overlap and when do they force themselves on others is a rather difficult process to capture, but in studying the micro-physics of power, one can possibly get a sense of which way political and cultural discourses are flowing.

The book is divided into nine sections, each focusing on an

important area in Indian politics. The first section on Education maps the various changes in higher education, within which the beginning of private universities and importance given to professional education is one factor that stands out, after the 1990s. What has been the import of this change? The essays here point to the new kind of 'brain drain', where young and promising students are increasingly pushed into 'glorified clerical' jobs, in the name of corporatisation. This is happening by giving a new meaning to elitism that is marked by forced social separation, indifference and suspended sense of normativity. These markers have in turn influenced the idea of quality education and the very idea of merit. The technocratic sense that they can been quantified, and this gets reflected in the anxiety initiated by global rank(l)ing of universities. The question however is how one would quantify social justice and the nascent knowledge systems, ideas that are finding their place in the curriculum and campus cultures, across the country. On the other hand, these social hierarchies that are being pushed down the education system also get expressed in the way courses get structured, including the social sciences. For instance, the endemic distinction that is maintained between theory and the empirical in the discipline of political science is a reflection of this social hierarchy. In fact, there could well be a social segregation between who chooses what. Education remains an important part of culture, and how we manage and structure higher education influences the larger meaning-making process.

Religion for long has remained the core essence of culture in the Indian context. It would be interesting to draw links between the phenomenon of rising Godmen and the response of *aam admi* to such imperatives, or with the culture of superstardom and personality-cult in politics. It could well be that it is more the compulsion to believe and empower one's self through the feeling of trust and faith, rather than anything specific with these phenomenon itself. Similarly, with entrenched caste-psyche, it could be debilitatingly limiting for oppositional politics because of its inherent dimension of unleashing the 'search for the weak', that could get reflected in questioning the powerful but also in its refusal to share its own entrenched power. When power relations cut both ways, it is often difficult to make sense of which way politics is flowing. Identity politics in India have always posed this difficult question for political observers. For instance, the recent discourse of moving beyond identity politics into a paradigm of governance is not a simple story of a linear flow but a complex story where self-perception in moving beyond identity actually entrenches and legitimises identity politics even more strongly. Similarly, self-perception of middle classes in India that they are champions of liberal idea of politics, that includes openness and dialogue further allows them to become self-righteous about their political choices, and further justify the exceptionalism of the state. Within this context, some of the essays raise the question of the changing nature of subaltern politics in India.

Subaltern politics in India have made difficult choices in order to stay afloat. Again, they have always remained open to be signified in multiple and often in contrasting ways. For instance, with the question of the formation of Telangana, one could argue that as it was subverting the domination of Coastal Andhra and the grip of its speculative capital, it was also getting increasingly communally polarised and was desperate to play the catching-up game. How does one sympathise with a just cause of formation of a separate state of Telangana, and yet highlight the point that smaller states have been spaces of speculative capital formation, and spatially entrenched in the global capital dynamics? Somewhat similar has been the story of the rise of anti-graft movements, they occur in the interstices and the very spaces created by neoliberalism. They seem to get resignified in ways they were not imagined in their original sense. For instance, promulgation of RTI, the initiative by Anna Hazare and AAP all seemed to have contributed to gradually undermining public institutions and giving space to private initiatives, as much as the rise of personality-cult of the 'Modi phenomenon'. Similarly, progressive and democratic-secular politics too fructified into entrenching the process of 'secular sectarianism' that seems to have contributed to the growth of majoritarian polity. The recent trend of a growing shift of the Dalit-Bahujan politics towards the right is one such unmistakable phenomenon. The recent political discourse by many representing these politics is that of the distinction between left, right and centre make little sense for the subaltern politics in India. This kind of a new articulation seems to be contributing to the rise of new binary of Left-Brahmin and Right-Bahujan in Indian politics, which is nothing short of turning the momentum in democracy on its head. In turn, this has both contributed and halted the rise of Left-of-centre politics in India. These unchartered territories need further reflection in order to make sense of what goes in the name of Indian politics.

Political parties have remained at the centre stage of a democratic imaginary in India. With all the cynicism that they bring into politics, they have remained exponentially relevant to the way subaltern groups have imagined mobility and change. The increasing voter turnouts in elections are a pointer in that direction. They have forged new political strategies, in spite of a state that looks increasingly non-responsive to their demands. Could one conclude that voters in India have learnt to reject but have little to choose from? Has this been made possible because of the consensus around the modern story of growth and development, and little being available by way of an alternative? Or is it that the neoliberal reforms have made it all that difficult to articulate the question of inequality because it is being imagined in terms of relative mobility, within the context of a perceived idea of ever-widening opportunity? Has it landed us in a new kind of 'politics without opposition'?

These essays have attempted, in a very preliminary sense, to reflect with a sense of urgency that many of these issues need. If they even manage to highlight the sense and direction of these processes, it should be considered as a worthwhile exercise.

A.G.
Delhi

EDUCATION

1

Tailored for the Corporates?

Higher education in India is undergoing a rapid transformation with increasing professionalisation and privatisation of courses, and an accompanying declining importance to conventional studies in social sciences and even natural sciences. There are optimists and votaries of some of these changes but there are also sceptics and critics, cautioning us of the adverse impact of this transformation. How should we understand this change?

We could at least partially make sense of these changes if we attempt to analyse the contribution of the national law schools, which are the latest addition to professional education alongside the Indian Institutes of Technology and the Indian Institutes of Management. There are already thirteen premier law schools in the country — in Bangalore, Hyderabad, Kolkata, Bhopal, Jodhpur, Raipur, and Kochi, among others. They have undoubtedly transformed the quality and status of legal education. From being often the last career option, law has become the first choice of some of the brightest students in India. How do these institutions work and what is it that they have contributed in the last decade or so? Having worked at the National University of Juridical Sciences, Kolkata, and then at the National Law School of India University, Bangalore (referred to as the Harvard of the East), these are some of the personal reflections and experiences I have had.

The first thing that struck me was the difference of these law schools from the conventional universities in terms of work culture, performance orientation, transparency, and freedom or autonomy with responsibility. In terms of teaching and evaluation, law schools have invented a unique set of mechanisms. The basis of this is transparency and equality in the teacher-student relationship. Students enjoy a lot of freedom in classrooms and most of the classes are expected to be highly interactive rather than just a monologue. Students more often than not differ with the view of the teacher. In fact, the entire course is divided into modules and then into sub-topics, which are given as project topics right at the beginning of the trimester or semester. Students are required to research and extensively read on their topics. At any time in the class, you have at least one student who is well informed about the topic the teacher is dealing with. Teachers become extremely accountable and performance invariably becomes the only criterion to 'survive.' More interestingly, at the end of the term, there is a detailed evaluation by the students on the subject knowledge, communication skills, and fairness of the teacher. Evaluation is taken seriously in both promoting and dispensing with the faculty. There have been innumerable occasions when faculty members were dispensed with on the basis of poor evaluation.

Added to this is the transparency and accountability in evaluation and examination of the pupils. Teachers are required to give in their question papers for the end term right at the beginning to make sure that they put in extra effort to cover the entire syllabus. Once the examinations are over, answer scripts are returned to the students and model sets of answers kept in the library for them to consult. Even after the examination process is over, students can seek consultation with the teachers to reason out marks they got. This demands a close, responsible and unbiased scrutiny on the part of the teachers.

Likewise, students are also required to work hard. They do 30-40 courses in pursuing their integrated five-year B.A. LLB (Honours) degree. They enjoy very little vacation. The trimester system (in Bangalore) for instance makes sure there is no vacation for more than 60 days in a year. Even during that period, students are sent on placement with various law firms to learn the practical aspects of lawyering. Outside the classroom, students are kept busy with various extra-curricular activities, apart from moot courts, that generate a deep sense of involvement among them. This was evident from the fact that the National Law School at Bangalore was selected in the very first year to compete in the Jessop international mooting contest in the United States. Students are expected to work for nothing less than 12-15 hours a day and teachers are in the university well before 9 a.m. They continue to work even after 6 p.m. This perhaps is unheard of in any conventional university.

Another very refreshing aspect about the law schools is the absence of a lethargic administration, which is unfortunately more powerful than the academics in the conventional university system. Faculty willingly takes part in some of the administrative work. Neither the Director nor the Registrar has personal staff. This partially has been responsible for a clean and scam-free administration, especially at the NLSIU. In fact, right from the time the law school was established and starved for funds, no donations were accepted and no one could influence the authorities to secure a seat. The admission procedure is completely transparent. Undoubtedly in a country suffering from appalling work culture and failure in the realisation of obligations towards institutions, law schools have put in place a new set of mechanisms and practices that are inspiring.

The other side of the story, however, is that these institutions are privatised and students pay heavy tuition fees to get trained. Therefore, we need to ask ourselves—is it possible or even desirable to extend and universalise this model of education? This is where we need to look at the flip side of this experiment.

Despite it having been a challenge to teach a bright set of students each year, I have throughout felt that they were socially a disengaged lot. Even what was being taught to them in their law classes was not socially or politically contextualised. Law is reduced to a 'technical' subject without any serious discussion on its social implications. Case laws are presented as though they exist in a vacuum and what is projected as relevant are only the 'facts of the case.' Statutes are represented as codifications of eternal and natural principles. This highly technocratic and socially insensitive approach goes well with the corporate requirements for which students are trained. Their entire education is moulded in accordance with job requirements and there is very little that is academic. Students develop an extremely pragmatic attitude towards both their teachers and the subjects. They distance themselves from anything that is emotional and requiring social empathy. Relationships between the students themselves appear to be driven by a sense of extreme competitiveness and indifference. There is an absence of a culture of cooperation and sharing. Student bodies seldom address any political or social issues. Issues that are highly local and campus-specific bog them down. These attitudes are prevalent because they perceive themselves more as 'consumers' in a market, rather than as students who are in pursuit of discovering newer facets of life. Needless to say, such a value-system goes well not only with the corporate houses that recruit them but also with the ideas of 'professionalism' and 'excellence.'

There is almost a hundred per cent placement for the students once they pass out. Most of them are absorbed by various corporate houses as legal officers or by law firms to draft reports for a case. However students themselves often accept that most of the jobs are not challenging and are monotonous. But what attracts some of the best students in India is the high pay they begin to draw at a fairly young age. This in many ways is a revised version of the 'brain drain.' Some of the best minds are drawn into an entirely uncreative work. This is also perhaps the greatest damage MNCs are doing to the nation —more than what they seem to be doing to the economy.

The challenge for the institutions of higher education really is: how do we incorporate the work ethic and transparency these institutions of professional education have established, without the accompanying consumerist and pragmatic culture? What are the alternative values and symbols that can motivate students and teachers to work hard? How do we reconcile the need to study for jobs with an academic and genuinely inquisitive learning? Unless these issues are addressed, we might end up with conventional universities without a work culture and professional institutions without social relevance. This to my mind is nothing short of a crisis in higher education

Published in *The Hindu*, November 2, 2004.

2

Ranking Universities: Comparing Harvard Apples with JNU Oranges

Indian academe is anguished that not a single Indian university has made it to the top 200 universities of the world in the recent *Times Higher Education* rankings. However, the debate so far has missed many points.

First, any discussion of evaluation of global educational standards and rankings cannot ignore the vast disparities in resources between the rich and poor parts of the world. An overwhelmingly large part of global knowledge production is concentrated in the developed world.

In 2009, Drexel University president Constantine Papadakis was the highest paid university president in America with an annual compensation of $49,12,127. That is around Rs. 27 *crore* for running a university! Even the highest-paid public university president earned nearly $2 million as salary in 2011.

The endowment of Harvard University is around $31 billion — more than 1/4 th of the GDP of Tamil Nadu. Research support in developed countries runs into hundreds of millions. As *Times* itself recognises, "income is crucial to the development of world-class research."

Most in the U.S.

Is it then surprising that of the top 200 universities, 76 are in the United States and 196, no less, in the developed countries (two from China, and one each from South Africa and Brazil are the only ones from the developing countries)? [76 from the U.S. and 196 in all from the developed countries. This includes the 76 from the U.S.] The crisis afflicting universities is thus, not an

Indian phenomenon alone, but generalised across the "Third World."

Second, while resources are crucial, they should not become an excuse for the abysmal standards of Indian universities. Instead the debate has to be extended, from merely technical solutions like establishing comprehensive universities or addressing student-teacher ratio, to the kind of academic culture that we have nurtured.

On Merit and Representation

Universities, on the one hand, have to reflect social reality by representing caste, class and gender criteria in order to overcome these hierarchies in academia. Academic freedom and egalitarian relations in the departments are expected not only to foster academic brilliance but also a socially progressive culture.

On the other, given the excessively communitarian nature of society, universities have, only in name, provided representation to disadvantaged sections. They have not actually overcome predisposed social hierarchies. Our academic culture is marked by patronage and networks or by bureaucratic hierarchies of seniority and administrative positions.

Even new political mobilisations around caste and reservations have focused only on the issues of representation without raising those of pedagogy and curriculum. There is a stalemate between merit and adequate representation.

In fact, those demanding reservations should have argued that reservation brings diversity, which develops new knowledge systems and new modes of understanding. This would, eventually, also contribute to a new institutional culture. Instead, inclusion of newer marginalised groups has only created parallel networks and patronage in defence against the existing ones of the dominant groups.

This kind of social breakdown has rarely contributed to new ideas and energies. Experimental culture has for long been supplanted by a culture of fear and insecurity, not merely among the new entrants, but also among "meritorious" social groups.

Top-down Syndrome

In fact, anything new is looked at sceptically, and often succumbs to the tyranny of age. Age-related hierarchy is perhaps the worst in the Indian university system and the least-debated sacred cow. The top-down syndrome has resulted in universities' resistance to introducing student evaluation of faculty, continued cases of victimisation of students—including sexual harassment and arbitrary evaluation, and consequently, lack of motivation among the students, translating into ills like rampant plagiarism.

Third, while Indian universities seek excellence, treating exercises such as the *Times'* ranking as sacrosanct is also problematic. Can we compare universities from America to Somalia? How do we arrive at an average from the vastly different material realities and the different starting points (which are historically and, often, violently determined) of these locations?

Faults

The *Times'* claims that it accounts for these disparities by providing a "comprehensive and balanced" comparison. But what does "international outlook" (one of the categories in *Times* worth 7.5 per cent) mean for a poor university in the global South which struggles to attract students even from the hinterlands of its own country? Or how does it go about achieving excellence in research, worth 30 per cent, and measured in terms of volume, income and reputation when the public spending on education is abysmally low?

The *Times'* rankings of 13 performance indicators also have no place for intangible features. In a university such as Jawaharlal Nehru University, students from some of the most backward regions study, thanks to its system of deprivation points. Students with very poor primary education, linguistic and writing skills, in very little time, gather confidence and become highly motivated, and look for an institutional culture that can translate this into a rigorous academic exercise. This is because of the vibrant student politics and a dominant discourse of social justice. Under what ranking can this amazing social feat of providing wide opportunity and social skills be judged?

While the poor quality of Indian universities is lamentable, does the solution lie in emulating the developed countries where high academic standards are now negated by the degenerating commercialisation of education? Thus students pay an annual fee of $40,000 for a bachelor's degree in an American Ivy League institution, and the average student-loan debt of 2011 in the U.S. was $26,500, rendering them perpetual bonded labourers of the market.

Students are not trained to become critical thinkers, but foot soldiers of the establishment. Therefore, they graduate without pondering over what it means when the university gives its presidents multimillion dollar salaries and its janitors $7 per hour. It is in this culture that people like Papadakis are able to double student enrolments and generate revenue surpluses rivalling multinational corporations.

Ultimately, the ranking debate is not just about Indian universities entering "the top 200," but also the need for a radically new academic culture, reducing inequalities of global academia, the ends of education, and the limitations of the ranking exercise itself.

Published in *The Hindu*, December 27, 2012.
(co-authored with Nissim Mannathukarren)

3

Social Sciences: A Case for De-Structuring Political Science

The teaching and research in political science has over the last few decades grown exponentially and greatly broadened its areas of study. However, this expansion has continued to be plagued by certain stubborn intellectual and epistemic problems that seem to be specific to the discipline of political science, even as they are not completely absent from other disciplines. One of the core problems that the discipline has failed to overcome in all these years has been one of what the Rudolphs have 'deplored (as) the deep and enduring split between theory and empirical research in political science' (Rudolph and Rudoplh, 2009, p. 139). I have elsewhere argued that

> Both 'theoretical imperialism' and the massive confusion between empiricism (including source fetishism of some disciplines) and the 'empirical mode of intellectual practice' has pushed political scientists to draw artificial self-referential boundaries and give up the study of societies in their manifold interconnections for 'specialised' and 'regionally enclosed' studies. (Gudavarthy, 2011, p. 120)

This, in other words, is what the Rudolphs refer to as a 'problem-driven' mode of approaching the subject-matter, rather than artificially slicing up the subject into very narrow areas of specialisation. Much of what is pursued as political theory or philosophy in India has very scant reference to concrete historical and sociological references; in fact, most scholars who work in this area assume that many empirical details are taken care of by rich theoretical frames. This assumption has reflection not merely in their research but in fact influences much of the teaching programmes across universities. Students trained in abstract philosophical systems rarely get tested in their ability to understand the nuances of social and political history of India. Theory is pursued as a self-enclosed specialisation, almost resonating what almost resonating what Kosambi (2002, p. 59) had observed with regard to Marxism, that it is a mode of thinking and 'not a substitute to thinking'. The assumption that pursuit of theory is of a higher order, as against empirical research, also resonates almost a caste/varna-system type of hierarchisation.[2]

The problem, however, is not one-sided; much of scholarship in the area of what is often referred to as 'Indian Politics' is bereft of rich theoretical categories. It has been mostly descriptive. As philosophers take pride in their lack of depth in empirical details, those belonging to the domain of 'Indian Politics' keep respectable distance from theory. Theoreticism and empiricism are then close 'colonial cousins' that continue to plague the discipline of political science in India.[3] Further, within the pursuit of 'Indian Politics', it is structured along the lines of specialisation in the study of institutions, processes and policy. Even here, those studying institutions rarely evince interest in political process; they assume institutions are best studied for what they are—being insular. Institutions are taught and researched along the line of exploring their internal rules, organisational structure—at the undergraduate level it goes by the unforgettable name 'powers and functions'—procedures, among others. The fact that institutions operate in a given social and political context has remained mostly under-researched, leave alone their interface with discursive/theoretical categories. Many of these studies on institutions, though well documented, have led to very few rich theoretical debates within the discipline of political science.

The most glaring fall-out of this can be analyzed in the context of the decline of public administration as a discipline in Indian academics. It began with a promise to work at the interface of theory (of state) and concrete application (for policy making). Had it achieved this goal it would, perhaps, have been one of the most creative areas of study. However, given the context of this endemic divide between theory and empirical/ concrete analysis it could achieve neither. It failed to develop a more relevant theorisation of Indian state and was not taken seriously by the policy makers. It was faced with the confusion as to how to handle political analysis once we step out of normative concerns integral to theory and yet not get reduced to mere empiricism of policy making. It got reduced to being dependent on the tools of management studies, and focused on organisational theory without any interface with the complex political, economic and cultural dynamics of the society.[4]

Further, at another level, the experiments to introduce inter-disciplinary approach have remained a non-starter in India. There is a deep discomfort from pedagogic methods to recruitment for teaching positions in the colleges and universities. In what ways can 'economic history' inform the study of contemporary 'Indian politics', or how the study of political theory can inform the formulation of economic policies, have remained clearly underdeveloped as areas of research.[5] Economics remains too technical, political theory too abstract, and history too detailed and cumbersome. Inter-disciplinarity has remained a no-man's land, and clearly not an easy problem to overcome. The only solace being that it is certainly not a problem specific to India but in fact has assumed global proportions. Reflecting on this, Frederic Jameson argues that

> professionalisation of the social sciences (thus) reinforces empiricist and anti-theoretical prejudices.... How can he (the philosopher—*my addition*) write on the French Revolution? He's no historian, he uses only secondary sources! How can he write on the history of French-unions and anarcho-syndicalism? He's no labour historian! How can he write on French Malthusianism and France's peculiar economic development? He's no economic historian. And as for Chinese deforestation and the gold and silver of the Spanish New world—it's obvious that a philosopher has no expertise on any of these subjects. (Jameson, 2009, p. 224)

There is clearly a pressing need to de-structure political science as it is taught and researched. The teaching programmes across universities should, to begin with, actively discourage the bifurcation of courses along the artificial borders between political theory, Indian Politics and International Relations. It, perhaps, would not be a bad idea for courses to be restructured and co-taught, to begin with. Political theory, in India, needs to be taught with an acute awareness of its own sociological and historical specificities; 'Indian politics' has to be taught with its backward–forward linkages between process, institutions and policy, and International Relations needs to be taught with some philosophical underpinnings, and not a mere cursory dialogue on the links between domestic and foreign policy.[6]

Further, research by young students at MPhil and PhD levels need to be encouraged with new methodology and at this suggested interface. This could include use of archival material, census data, ethnography, alongside (and not in lieu of) rich theoretical frames. For instance, those pursuing election studies in India need to be equipped with theoretical debates on mode of production and passive revolution, and those pursuing philosophy need to step outside, dirty their hands in the messy details of 'Indian Politics', lest theory would remain normative and politics empiricist in nature. The former will lead to 'imperialism of categories', while the latter will only result in 'fundamentalism of experience'. This has to be a bottom-up process, de-structuring the unhealthy divide that has come to structure the discipline with provincial universities teaching mostly simple-minded 'Indian politics' and metropolitan centres such as Delhi will continue to offer uncontaminated theory.7 The provincial centres would require accessible reading material in political theory that bears meaning to local reality, including wide-scale translation of existing material in English into various Indian languages.[8] As a corollary process, those in the metros need to mandatorily learn one Indian language, if not more.[9] It would not, perhaps, be a bad idea to have a stronger exchange programmes between metropolitan and provincial universities, for both the faculty and the students, instead of a single-minded pursuit of exchange programmes between Indian and mostly European and North American universities (not even those universities in other southern continents figure as part of these exchange programmes).

De-mystifying theory is only possible if we can also break down the fundamentalism of experiential epistemology. For instance, it could be an interesting issue to debate for political scientists, if students coming from specific states and regions need to be necessarily encouraged to work on their own societies, or would it be intellectually challenging to ask them to take up more comparative research agendas and areas for fieldwork? This kind of inter-regional research, given the nature of diversity in India, will in itself, perhaps, augment theoretical engagement, since they need to speak to a reality that is not only different but also might be at odds with their settled understanding of political processes. The nature of this theory, however, could be one that is located—as against 'speaking from nowhere'.[10] Otherwise, I feel, much of research has become constrainingly conformist, even as it claims to be critical.[11] The debate on the discipline needs to be now acutely aware of the need to shift from an old episteme (artificial discontinuities, hierarchical, self-enclosed, over specialisation) that has guided and ordered much of the research till date, to a new episteme (thematic focus, non-hierarchical, inter-disciplinary and multi-method mode) that awaits its turn.

NOTES

1. It, in fact, would not be a bad idea to study the social backgrounds of those who pursue theoretical research in India. I, for one, would guess that they might mostly belong to the higher echelons of the social location, and this might need some explanation, and some thinking as to what can be done about it as a correction to the pedagogic methods pursued in the teaching and research of political theory/philosophy.
2. This problem is further compounded by inadequate linguistic skills in reading, writing and teaching in English.
3. Professor Ram Reddy (former chairperson of the UGC), in course of personal communication, once observed that Sociology was a subject-matter in search of a discipline, and Public Administration was a discipline in search of subject-matter.
4. Even in a university such as Jawaharlal Nehru University that has been structured with a clear inter-disciplinary focus, the interaction between faculty members of various centres, or students opting for cross-over courses, is very slim.
5. International Relations as a sub-discipline has remained theoretically limited in its foundations, and therefore played second fiddle to the policy makers. Much of the scholarship only

endorsed the foreign policy imperatives in the name of 'national interest'. It could not step out of this prism that is foundational to the discipline, even if some scholars have questioned these assumptions of Morgenthau theoretically.

6. It is interesting in this context to observe that in much of south India Political Science is almost equated with International Relations. It remains the most popular branch. What could be the possible sociological reasons for these remains to be analysed. I guess, in much of the provincial north India, 'Indian Politics' has an edge over other areas, leaving theory/philosophy to a very few universities in the metropolitan cities, which thereby remain mostly without any concrete reference point. Much of post-colonial theory in India has come as a response to this divide and has to some extent provided a corrective frame. However, it is based on a rather exaggerated and unreflective eulogisation of the local, and the idea of community, and unproblematic celebration of the cult of the subaltern. I have dealt with some of this critique in a recent volume I edited (Gudavarthy, 2012).
7. It has always been my experience in presenting papers at seminars organised by provincial universities that many academics and students have keen interest in local politics, they have a lot of statistics and data on their fingertips, keen interest in institutional procedures of local bodies, information on personalities and their idiosyncrasies and how that influences policy making, among many other such fascinating aspects of pursuing a very organic mode of understanding what is otherwise an intellectualised project within the institutional frame. There is, however, little interest beyond that immediate into drawing generalisations, and speaking through 'categories' that might actually resonate or challenge their own understanding, reminding us of what Marx said about Feuerbach—sparks that fail to illuminate!
8. It could be useful to debate if this language could be preferably one other than their mother tongue.
9. For instance, this question of students taking up their own regions often emerges in JNU (though partly unjustified) with students coming from the north-eastern region. But the merit in this complaint is that much of persuasion by the faculty often fails to alter the conclusions that students begin to draw before they commence their research. This, I believe, is true of all other regions.
10. Being critical is not necessarily being non-conformist. Critical

analysis itself and the categories it produces, such as, privileging non-linear over linear, particular and local over universal, among others, could gain a hegemonic position, blocking the interrogation of formulations that come to represent critical analysis in contemporary times.

REFERENCES

Chattopadhyaya, B. and Kosambi, D.D. (2002). *Combined Methods in Indology and Other Writings.* D.D. Kosambi: Compiled, edited and introduced by Brajadulal Chattopadhyaya. New Delhi: OUP.

Gudavarthy, Ajay. (2011). Review of *Explaining Indian Democracy: A Fifty Year Perspective, 1956–2006* by Lloyd I. Rudolph and Susanne Hoeber Rudolph. *Indian Economic and Social History Review, XLVIII*(1), January–March, 117–120.

———. (2012). *Reframing Democracy and Agency in India: Interrogating Political Society*. London: Anthem.

Jameson, Frederic. (2009). *Valences of the Dialectic*. London: Verso.

Rudolph, Lloyd I. and Rudolph, Susanne Hoeber. (2009). *Explaining Indian Democracy: A Fifty Year Perspective, 1956–2006*. New Delhi: Oxford University Press.

Published in *Studies in Indian Politics*, December, 2013, Vol. 2

4

Law Schools and Elitism

Ajay Gudavarthy is an Assistant Professor at the Centre for Political Studies at the Jawaharlal Nehru University. Before joining JNU in 2006, he taught Political Science and Constitutional History at NUJS, Kolkata before shifting to NLSIU, Bangalore where he took courses on Political Obligation and Indian Politics. In this interview with Bar & Bench, *Gudavarthy talks about the forced elitism of national law schools, the stigmatisation of reservation and the new politics of the Aam Aadmi Party.*

Bar & Bench: *In 2001, you got your first teaching assignment at the National University of Juridical Sciences in Kolkata. Two years later, you shifted to National Law School, Bangalore where you taught Political Science. How were these experiences?*

Ajay Gudavarthy: Teaching at NUJS was very interesting; interesting in two senses. One, the students were extremely bright, so to teach social science to such a bright lot in India was itself a unique experience. In conventional universities, you really don't get that kind of quality [of students].

But the bigger challenge was also that [the students] were socially a bit removed. Some came from fairly elite backgrounds although when I actually began to enquire, I realised they were not from that kind of an elite background. But once they come on campus they almost imagined that they came from an elite background. And one of the markers of being elite, and this I noticed both at NUJS and NLSIU, was to be socially uprooted. I think it was a very conscious effort on the part of students to be socially removed. So it was an interesting teaching environment.

B&B: This is something you referred to in the piece you wrote for

The Hindu in 2004. How did you overcome this challenge?

AG: Well in the classroom you could raise various questions and issues because the students were bright. One could introduce complex text, raise the level of discussion, etc but the problem occurred when you wanted to connect it to reality. For instance, I used to teach political philosophy and students were happy to discuss Rawls. But if you said that Rawls' policy supported reservation, they would be completely against it. The entire class would say that they were opposed to reservation.

B&B: In the same piece, you also wrote about the remarkable levels of transparency in law school administration.

AG: Yes, NLSIU had an extremely transparent mechanism. Being the first [national law school] I think it started with some idea of building an institution of superlative success. I think Prof. Menon had that idea in mind. If you look at NLS in fact, it even had a tinge of academic orientation. Other law schools lacked a research component and for many of us this was a major disincentive.

B&B: In that same piece, you write that, "Relationships between the students themselves appear to be driven by a sense of extreme competitiveness and indifference."

AG: Yes and the problem is that this indifference was not really an organic indifference. In Indian law schools, there is this marker of being "elite". I think students were under tremendous pressure to maintain this attitude. Many students came from very middle class backgrounds and it was only a small, creamy section consisting of sons and daughters of leading lawyers, industrialists or bureaucrats. I think the tone and tenor was set by these elite.

B&B: And how did this elitism reflect itself? As a teacher, were these specific instances that you observed?

AG: When at NUJS for instance, I invited leading lawyer and civil rights expert, Dr. K. Balagopal for a talk. What do you expect from an institution when you are inviting such an individual, a leading human rights activist and a lawyer? There should be general curiosity at least.

I would expect that here in JNU, students would have come in large numbers, engaged with him and disagreed. But at NUJS it was a completely dull atmosphere and they did not know who he was. Even after introducing him, there was very little engagement. It was a kind of forced interaction almost. But you cannot compel students to question or to engage, can you?

It is very difficult to survive for too long in such an institution.

B&B: Thoughts on extremely competitive nature of law schools?

AG: This whole idea of being very competitive is one that drives them. And within students themselves as well, the inter-personal relations are very competitive.

B&B: Competition for what?

AG: Partly, as I said, it is very imaginary. And partly it is for these corporate jobs. They have these placement slots. If you are in the first five ranks, you get placed here, the next twenty ranks there, etc. It was quite overwhelming on campus. The only thing that really interested and motivated them outside of class was moot courts.

But again, this was almost always to add to their CVs and help them when they apply for jobs. The whole thing was very structured, very formalistic. "What adds to my CV?" is what they often ask themselves.

B&B: And how should it have been?

AG: You see the purpose why national law schools were started was because legal practice and legal education was in a bad shape in India. There was no academic spirit, no good students, etc but unfortunately these national law schools have become like a recruitment centre for corporates.

Many of my students are still in touch with me and I don't think they enjoy what they are doing. In that Hindu piece I have written that this is like a new kind of a brain drain. It is not that you are pulling them out of the country but within the country you are not giving them something challenging to do. They are undoubtedly a bright lot, but you are giving them glorified clerical posts in corporate firms.

Many of my students themselves feel that this is not very challenging, it is monotonous but then they also say that they feel trapped—some say they have educational loans for instance.

B&B: In a 2012 piece on the global ranking of educational institutions, you wrote, "[Student loans] render them perpetual bonded labourers of the market." Do you think Indian law schools also suffer from this?

AG: Yes, we are heading in that direction. Now one of the solutions is to put education outside the market. Education has to be funded by the state and not personally funded that too at such a high cost. Why should NLSIU or NUJS charge such high fees? Is there any justification for this?

And even if they want to raise funds from within, it has to be in proportion to who can afford, how much they can afford, what kind of students you require, etc.

But that is just a part of the problem. In my opinion, law schools represent one of the worst kinds of culture in higher education.

B&B: Why do you say that?

AG: Because of this entire idea of being elite. It is a very self-conscious move for institutions that are not elite by their social composition but want to look very elitist.

IITs have a natural sense of being elite institutions, so do IIM's. So students are more relaxed in these institutions. I have taught at some of them and the students would really engage in class. IIM students are socially very sensitive. There was a fair amount of interest, of being socially tuned. They know what is happening around them but you don't find that in law students at all.

And this is a very self-consciously taught idea of what it means to be elite. That you have to be socially removed, that every day things in society don't matter. Because elites in India define themselves by social separation—how different are they from the ordinary or how distinct they are. I think something somewhere went wrong with the law school experiment.

B&B: Do you think greater reservation is one possible solution?

AG: See you need reservation but the kind of pressure these students face in campus is terrible. I have personally known cases where reservations have been completely stigmatised, completely silenced; there is no open debate or rather there is just a single debate.

If you come to a campus like JNU, there are different voices; people are at least willing to listen to each other. If I look at my classes in JNU, students are willing to discuss several issues, there are agreements and disagreements.

B&B: And do you think this is directly due to JNU's reservation policies?

AG: Well it certainly affects the social composition. In JNU there is one section that is elite, which is strongly against reservation for instance. But you can see a change [in them] from the second semester onwards. The campus opens them up, they realise that there are other voices, why reservation policies exist, etc. And that makes the campus vibrant and I think education institutions must be vibrant.

B&B: Sticking with the reservation question, in a speech given in Osmania University, you said that the very debate of reservation is seen as a sort of "compromise" and that it is a very "Brahmanical understanding" of the issue at hand.

AG: My argument there was more on the way we are pursuing reservation. See reservation is necessary but what I was saying was that at a certain point, [reservation] is becoming counter productive. The idea that reservation and merit are dichotomised is something that needs to be relooked.

Those who get reservation also need to be meritorious in the system. It is not that reservation should mean that merit is bogus. Reservation is just enabling individuals to enter the system. But once you enter, you cannot say that there is nothing else left. The purpose of reservation is to realise one's highest potential.

B&B: How do you think reservations for students ought to be implemented? Should there be any changes in the current model?

AG: See the current model has the problem of protection until the students enter. But once they enter they do not have any enabling practices in the university. For example at JNU, many students come with linguistic challenges such as speaking English.

So you give them reservation, ask them to join the institution and then tell them to compete with the rest! And teachers are faced with a kind of dilemma every day. You know a student has certain problems but then how do you evaluate? You can't say, I will give him a good grade since he is from such and such caste. There are no institutional mechanisms to address these kinds of problems.

Also one should realise that it is not merely the University that contributes towards the student. If these students perform to their potential, they will contribute to the merit of the institution. They will expand the base of the institution. Some students come from remote areas. Suppose they bring information on new kinds of tribes—isn't that an expansion of the knowledge system?

So my argument in that speech was about combining reservation with merit. I argued that this combination actually leads to the expansion of the knowledge base. But this can only take place provided you have these institutional mechanisms in place.

Otherwise it will be an "either or" situation—either you have merit or you have reservation. And that is just stigmatising the student.

B&B: This is a completely separate issue but you have also written about judicial pronouncements. Do you think the judiciary also suffers from being far removed from reality?

AG: Reality—I don't know. I think judges carry their prejudices into to their judgment and one has to realise that. I don't think there is anything purely legal that works in the Indian context. I don't think they go purely by law as such but also by their political preferences. In fact I am pushing all my students to study this. Judgments will almost always be in tune with the political mood of the country. Very rarely will you have judgments that are not in tune with the popular mood of the country.

B&B: One last question unrelated to law schools—what is your opinion on Kejriwal and the AAP?

AG: See it's a new phenomenon as far as the institutional practices of election are concerned. They have introduced newcomers to fight election, internal accountability, the way they relate to the electorate—there is a whole bunch of electoral practices that are fairly new; which we always aspire for but nobody did it. To that extent, it's a new experiment.

But in terms of the politics of Kejriwal, it is again like the judiciary, you don't know where they stand. You have a Prashant Bhushan who takes a certain position on Kashmir to someone like Kumar Vishwas who has his own views on sexual minorities and women.

And they are taking the repeated argument that they will take position when they arrive at the situation or that they are post- ideological which I don't think is true. They have come up on the wave of anti-Congress wave that is happening. Corruption is a big issue but they have made it very symbolic. Today, they have framed it in such a way that everyone can draw whatever meaning they want from the idea of corruption.

For example, if you come to Vasant Kunj where I live not having enough parking space is corruption. They will say, "Corruption ke kaaran there is no proper planning. (There is no proper planning because of corruption)" If you go to the slum areas, inflation is because of corruption. That is the appeal of the AAP and why they have won in both posh colonies of South

Delhi as well as reserved constituencies. But how long can such symbolism be sustained?

B&B: Coming back to law schools, what are your thoughts on legal aid clinics?

AG: Menon had started that but they are all so formalistic. It is just one more thing to add to your CV. And you can see the clear hierarchy—the bright lot never go [for legal aid clinics]. It's the middle and lower lot who go for such programs, human rights (laughs) etc. You already have a varna system in law schools, you are already stigmatised within law schools.

Therefore, the whole attitude to education is very instrumental. Knowledge can never be instrumental. You can have links to the market but in law school it is completely reduced to an instrumentality. For any course a student will ask, "What do I get out of it?" or "What will my CV look like?" etc.

And then you have these internships, corporate firms in the fourth year, human rights in the second year. Worse, you will think that these two (corporate and human rights) are unrelated. And this is reflected in the curriculum itself. How is human rights unrelated to competition law? Or labour law unrelated to constitutional law? And these subjects are also taught like that; the faculty also imagines that this is the case. You take the brightest faculty, she will be teaching corporate law, the less bright, human rights. And the social sciences are even further reduced, further stigmatised (laughs).

You have to complete social science subjects in the first year itself—what kind of a bizarre logic is this? And that is where I had a lot of arguments with Prof. Menon. Can you understand Constitutional law without understanding colonial history? But in law school they can understand; they have this unique methodology of understanding everything by itself (laughs)

I think law concretises the entire human experience. Therefore every legal provision would have multiple links to sociology philosophy, history, ideas of justice, etc. But the way we have reduced teaching law in this country.

B&B: Are you a cynic?

AG: (*laughs*) Oh no, I am only reading the situation as it exists. It is not a question of cynicism. You need to have a different approach to teaching law. You cannot have this kind of instrumental approach where students are just not equipped to link things. Ask the average law student what is the link between social science and competition law. I doubt if they will actually find any meaning in that question.

Talk to students and you will know what are the courses they consider important or valuable. Why does this happen? Why this kind of hierarchy?

A good competition lawyer should also go for a sociological education. Any sociological study will tell you that all corporates have caste-based discrimination. Recently my colleagues conducted a number of interviews across several corporates and they discovered a completely silent exclusion of Dalits and OBCs. Now if a law school student is working in a corporate law firm or a corporate, how can s/he be bereft of or completely blind to this social phenomenon?

Obviously these are linked—how corporate law works is linked to what kind of society we are in. But I don't think law schools are equipping students to make these kind of linkages.

This interview was first published in *Bar and Bench* on February 7, 2014.

Culture and Community

5

Modernity and Godmen

The recent conviction of Asaram Bapu and his son Narayan Sai for alleged rape and sexual assault charges have once again brought to the forefront the culture of power and the way it is exercised over trusting followers. The catch, however, is not merely the breach of trust of the devotees but also the refusal of the followers to believe the mountain of evidence against their revered guru. This again is not the first time such a situation has emerged. Earlier we had incidents of young men found murdered in the ashram headed by Puttaparthi Sai Baba in Ananthpur and evidence against his claims to perform magic of presenting his devotees with gifts created out of thin air. Any amount of incriminating evidence does not seem to dither the followers and devotees of godmen, and they continue to invest their faith, trust and affection in them. The sociology of faith in a deeply divided and hierarchy/status-conscious society like ours needs deeper probing and public reasoning, even if this phenomenon looks beyond reason. Divided societies would have divided reasons; specific to their own social location, though externally it would like a following that has blind faith beyond any sociological causation. To begin with, in modern societies the very idea and feeling of investing hundred percent faith and trust in anything is itself a unique and a rewarding emotion. Modern society based on critical rationality and self-doubt also makes human beings restless who become like nomads with a deep sense of homelessness. The compulsion of unrelentingly pursuing one's own self-interest, in order to merely survive and get what is perceived to be one's due could be an exhausting experience for most; in that to find a faith, a resting-place could be very soothing. For the bulk of the population groups and the *common man* to find someone whom you could trust without second thoughts could be a very uplifting experience. Since complete faith is in itself a necessity, it is not easily given up even when you offer incriminating evidence because this can be accepted only at one's own peril: believing the evidence is as damaging to the followers as the guru himself.

Revolving Around the Self

To the affluent sections of the society, where the followers come from the higher echelons of caste and class, it is not so much about the need for faith but the dire need to protect their self-image of being distinguished and exceptional. The logic could be one where you follow a guru who is great and larger-than-life, and in following him, or realising that greatness one reassures one's self that he or she is also unique and exceptional. As modernity propels a process of homogenisation of social roles, while all along demanding uniqueness and laying premium on individuality, one might realise this in following a sect that is different from the run-of-the-mill religiosity. Reflected glory becomes a compulsive mode for ego-gratification, and recognising that the guru could be fallible also raises doubts about ones own exceptionality. It is also these sections of society that are looking for reasons and causation in one's life without locating them within a larger society; they need explanations and solutions that begin and end with themselves.

Much of the discourse of the religious cults of *babas* and gurus place the follower exclusively at the centre of their explanations as to why things happen the way they do. This gives both a sense of control over one's own life and also creates a justification for absolute trust in the guru. It is a reasoning that is pre-social, or for that matter post-social in nature, since society is looked as the cause or source of ordinariness, finding one's own self hyper-separated from the social domain looks highly gratifying. While modernity and the discourse of individualism augment hyper-separation of the self from the social, discourses of religiosity and spirituality provide a similar avenue with a social justification rooted in the reality of "our modernity". This also goes well with the new middle classes and their acquisitive nature that new market relations have shaped with their unrelenting encroachments into personal and cultural domains. Here too things begin and end with the self a neatly crafted and segregated entity that was otherwise lost in the crowd. This is precisely what Bertrand Russell had advocated as the source of unhappiness and argued in his celebrated classic *The Conquest of Happiness* that the real source of happiness lies in impersonal interests and curiosity to learn. Urban classes, it seems steadily have lost the capacity for both. They neither have a modern culture of hobbies, nor have they managed to retain traditional respect for knowledge. Instead, the cultural milieu is one against experimentation, which suspends into a mode of self-denial, wherein what one does not know either does not exist or is irrelevant. This creates a deep sense of vacuum in much of social life, sucks meaning out of social and even personal interactions and opens up the everyday life to a deadly combination of insecurity and predictability. The sheer banality of everyday life has to resort to a belief in *magic and mantras*; they serve the purpose of providing entertainment and quick-fix solutions (that goes well with the culture of making quick-money). Dancing and singing by the gurus provide the much sought relief from a highly disciplined and regulated life.

Faith and the *Aam Aadmi*

The scores of poor and marginalised who come to the gurus seem to find in them a mode of bridging the class and social exclusion that they experience as a routine. The performative meetings/spectacles held by the gurus emerge as new social spaces shared with the well-to-do, allowing them to reclaim a residual assertion of dignity and perceive a degree of social visibility and inclusion. Unlike the traditional religiosity of visiting a temple, the lively aspect of seeing a real-time godman in flesh and blood could be empowering and offer a dose of self-confidence that is in massive scarcity in societies like ours. Breaching this formidable social logic and undercurrent could well be of a different order from condemning and finding a mountain of evidence against godmen. The value of symbolism in the performative dimension for the *common man*, or in more recent parlance *aam aadmi*, is then not just restricted to the cultural domain but could transpire in the political domain as well. To get past or even negotiate with this symbolism in the political, one has to comprehend its source in the psycho-cultural domain.

At one end as "aam admi" is susceptible to symbolism, at the other end of the spectrum, the dominant notions of power are reinforced in the extra-institutional domain. While leading spiritual gurus like Sri Sri Ravishankar reiterate the need to privatise education so that people realise its importance and thereby a meritocratic order is restored, sacred pilgrim sites such as Tirupathi work through given notions of social capital and connections. A visit to Tirupathi will allow one to realise how its daily operations are based on connections with ministers (VIP *darshan* is made possible through the recommendation of the minister of endowment or the chief minister's office), and there is a self-evident display of social status and money. These everyday practices in the psycho-cultural domain reinforce the dominant notions of power in the political domain. It is therefore not surprising why Narendra Modi, with his aggressive posturing and masculine image looks *powerful*, and why the likes of Rahul Gandhi seem uninitiated and lethargic. The dominant and the dominated, governed and those governing, the elite and the subaltern are inextricably linked through the same socio-cultural practices, disallowing not only claims to an "autonomous domain" but also making it difficult to unabashedly celebrate the cult of the subaltern. This then is an agenda as much for the political activists as cultural torch-bearers in India.

Published in the *Economic and Political Weekly* (Web Exclusives)
Vol. XLIX, No. 3, January 18, 2014.

6

Cinema and Superstardom

Sometimes, looking for an explanation for hard-to-understand aspects of society becomes necessary when these say something about ourselves—and our compulsive necessity to create the inexplicable. And Rajnikant's journey to superstar and veritable demi-god is one such social phenomenon, one that's escaped many an analysis. What can explain this larger-than-life experience?

I can think of three possible, if partial, explanations.

Firstly, Rajnikant's celebrated style, and the "antics" that are so characteristic of it—the flip of his cigarette, the twist of his goggles. These are not merely style statements; they are also socially subversive acts. While his ease with sunglasses subverts class symbols, his use of cigarettes dignifies "mass" symbols. Often doing them together creates a strong effect within the confined social space of a cinema hall.

Secondly, Rajnikant has a distinct body language, and a mode of projecting it that is unusual and therefore powerful. His side glance, his twist of the fist, his rather awkward style of sitting cross-legged, to mention a few, exude a rare energy and confidence—a person at ease with himself. In a segregated society that is at best judgmental, and at worst prejudicial, both the art of being at ease with oneself and the science of self-confidence and self-esteem are denied to most individuals. It is an indulgence; few can afford to refuse to be socially conditioned, to live by the terms they set. In cinema and real life, body language such as Rajnikant's is a rarity: it allows you to lower your guard, without the threat of losing your sense of the self or your self-esteem.

In a caste-ridden society where the colour of one's skin, one's dress sense and eating etiquette, and one's choice of profession are all under scrutiny, this provides on-screen relief. It is almost like licence to behave—to speak, think and gesticulate—as one would like.

Finally, there is something very distinct about the relation between his on-screen and off-screen images. They are completely disjointed—and, in addition, there appears no anxiety to cover that up. This lends inexplicable authenticity to his over-the-top on-screen characters and performances. He is known to be simple and honest; his lifestyle is modest; he remains a vegetarian and sleeps on the floor, keeping luxury at arms' length, in spite of being the highest-paid actor in the country.

Nor does he hide his modest background as a bus conductor in Bangalore; indeed, every story about him begins with that fact, and ends with his current demi-god status. He comes across, and looks, unbelievably different in real life from what he does on-screen—calm, polite and, of course, bald.

He began his career in films with negative roles, as a villain, and before moving centrestage as an iconic hero. And throughout he has come across as unfazed by changes, and thus authentic. The only actor who shared some of this was Raajkumar, the matinee idol of the Kannada cinema industry, known for his austere persona and lifestyle.

And both Rajnikant and Raajkumar maintained a respectable distance from the arena of active politics. In complete contrast, stars such as NTR and MGR nurtured larger-than-life-images in real life as well; they were overwhelming and overbearing, benevolent and glad to extend feudal patronage. Rajnikant is none of these, and therefore his public persona is at odds with the demands of an active political life. While Rajnikant represents himself in a film to entertain his fans, NTR and MGR re-presented themselves on-screen as what they were supposed to be in real life.

In a context where directors exploit the star's off-screen images—whether of Salman Khan as brutish, loud and impulsive, for his character as Chulbul Pandey in *Dabangg*, or Sanjay Dutt as gullible and emotional for his character as

Munnabhai—to create an authentic on-screen image, here is a person who creates an on-screen image that is genuine precisely because he is not that character, but simply someone who intends to entertain. He, therefore, succeeds in doing that like no one else.

Published in *The Indian Express*, October 1, 2010.

7

Identity versus Governance

One of the key issues that have occupied the imagination of the electorate in the general elections in 2014 is the tension in Indian democracy between identity and governance. Most of the political parties, especially the national parties, were claiming to have moved to a governance paradigm as against the mobilisation of social groups on the basis of a 'narrow' identity. Congress claims to have introduced a new discourse on 'good governance' with the introduction of economic reforms, BJP under Narendra Modi is projecting governance to induce growth, prosperity and higher GDP as a solution to many evils plaguing the nation, and finally, more recently the newly formed AAP is claiming to have introduced a post-identity and post-ideology politics to strengthen democracy by way of foregrounding corruption as an issue concerning all castes, classes and regions. What exactly was the problem with identity politics? Identity politics that have had an exponential growth in the last two decades in Indian democracy, while it managed to mobilise the marginalised they seem to have ushered piece-meal changes, introduced competitive mobilisation between different social groups leading to sectarianism, and identity-fetishism. This has lead to creation of new social elites among the hitherto marginalised social groups such as the Dalits, and the Muslims, leaving behind the bulk of population in whose name the specific identity groups are mobilised. It is these elites who then make demands of their own, such as the need for 'Dalit Capitalists', unmindful of the fact that the nature of such an economy would exploit Dalit labour more than anybody else. Further, identity politics entrench patron-client relations between the social elites of the respective identity groups and the rest of the population belonging to those identities. The worst outcome of sustained identity mobilisation has been proliferation of intra-subaltern conflicts as we have witnessed between the various sub-castes among the Dalits in Andhra Pradesh, between the Dalits and the OBCs as witnessed in Khairlangi, or between the OBCs and the Muslims as witnessed in the recent riots in Muzzafarnager. These intra-subaltern conflicts are not only replacing the conflict with elites, within and outside their respective groups, but are also making an alliance with social elites possible or rather a necessity to win elections, as is clear from the shift in the language of BSP from Bahujan to Sarvajan, making an uncanny alliance between the Dalits and Brahmins a viable electoral strategy in Uttar Pradesh. Finally, identity politics have failed to deliver material benefits and open up wide-scale economic opportunities, and instead have propelled symbolic mobility and psychological empowerment, of the kind we witnessed with the symbolism of Mayawati, (for instance installing statues of Ambedkar) and Lalu Prasad Yadav of the RJD. While these contribute towards ideas of dignity, respect and a sense of the self, and remain important achievements in themselves but cultural mobility invariably leads to demands for a share in the economic resources. This can clearly be observed in the case of the Muslims, especially after the Sachar Committee Report, who are now demanding better educational and employment opportunities. In India, we are strangely witnessing a simultaneous rise of cultural assertion, and economic dispossession, which is what makes our democracy look chaotic and for some even unruly. It is for these reasons that there is a new consensus of sorts against the adverse impact of identity politics on Indian democracy among the upwardly mobile professional/urban classes, as well as the rural and urban poor.

While, one understands why the new language of Modi or AAP has come as a relief for many we need to ask two follow-up questions. Have political parties and their mobilisations in fact really moved beyond identity mobilisations? Is the alternative to identity politics to be found in the language of governance? First, it is a grave exaggeration if one were to believe that political mobilisation has unproblematically moved to a more universal governance paradigm from a 'sectarian' identity politics. Even a cursory look at all those political leaders who have come to symbolise discourse of governance will make it evident that it is laced with a 'liberal' dose of identity mobilisation. For instance, Nitish Kumar's governance is combined with sub-categorisation of the OBCs into EBCs and MBCs. Modi's corporate governance and growth-centric rhetoric is combined with a deeply polarising discourse against the minorities that he returns to when he alludes to the 'burqha of secularism', or his claims of being a 'Hindu Nationalist', or deliberately compares the minorities to 'puppies that have come under the wheels'. It is therefore untenable to imagine that the Modi of 2002 is very different from the Modi of 2012. It is not an explicit identity versus governance, as popular discourse has come to perceive but more of a certain combination of identity with the rhetoric of efficient governance. Similar is the case with AAP, it has made a pitch for the same similar shift to a more identity-blind transparent and accountable governance, and also cited this as its mobilisational strategy for the elections in Delhi; the most cited case being Shazia Ilmi, a Muslim, contesting from a Hindu-dominated constituency (though it is a different matter that it was a one-off case of a prominent face of AAP losing the elections). Whether it is the composition of the new Ministry of AAP or the nature of polling where many surveys have found Muslims voting in a much smaller number for AAP compared to others because there weren't too many Muslim faces in the party, the identities have not really died out. Identity claims have only moved from claiming exclusive cultural dignity to attempting to combine that with new types of economic opportunities. It is evident in the case of Gujjars demanding the status of STs, or Rajputs wanting to be listed as OBCs. The issue here is not mobility in ritual hierarchy but a share (legitimate or otherwise) in state resources.

Finally, is the alternative to the ills of identity politics to be sought in governance, if it means an exclusive growth-centric strategies that India began with during the phase of liberalisation in the 1990s, which prompted Rob Jenkins to refer to it as 'reforms by stealth'. It has since then moved to a judicious or otherwise combination of reforms with social welfare policies, such as the Right to Food Security, Land Acquisition Bill, Street Vendors Bill, apart from the MGNREGA, riding on which Congress came back to power in 2009. Or for that matter the governments of Chhattisgarh and Madhya Pradesh have been voted back in the recent elections in 2013 in recognition of the spate of welfare policies that were put in place. Governance as growth has very marginally translated into a trickle-down for the poor, and therefore the need to have more pronounced social welfare policies in place. Having said this it must be recognised that in spite of ushering a spate of welfare policies the scene for Congress is rather bleak, precisely because it seems to have failed in delivering and implementing these policies through effective-governance strategies. It lacked transparency and accountability and got caught in a series of high-level scams, which not only makes the government inefficient but also look arrogant in a mood of 'participatory democracy' that we are witnessing. Strangely similar is the case with Left-of-Centre political parties, such as the CPI and CPM that have continued to raise issues of poverty, ill-effects of FDI for the marginalized, landlessness and displacement but could neither creatively plug into identity mobilisation nor particularly look accountable and open for dialogue and participatory ethos, which partly explains their declining presence in electoral calculations. This, however, does not mean that we move back to an exclusive growth-centric governance paradigm, rather the road ahead is a choice between governance combined with a polarised polity and governance combined with a social-democratic welfare agenda that is inclusive of all particular social identities such as the Dalits, OBCS, minorities and women. Identities cannot be undermined or brushed aside, nor can they simply be mobilised for cultural assertion any more without including a concrete and tangible programme of economic empowerment, while governance cannot simply mean growth any more but the way it contributes through a discourse of accountability, institutional procedures and transparency for widening economic opportunities and a more inclusive-democratic order.

Published in *The Hindu*, January 24, 2014.

8

Debating the Secular-Communal Divide

Come election time and we invariably indulge in India's very own 'Great Debate' on the secular-communal divide in Indian democracy. While the Left and regional parties that wish to either launch the third front or align with the Congress resort to the need to keep communal forces at bay and maintain the secular fabric of the nation, and BJP and Sangh Parivar lament minority appeasement and vote-bank politics and instead suggest universal development and providing education and employment to all: 'Justice to all, appeasement of none' or 'Sabka Saath, Sabka Vikas' is their new mantra. In terms of popular perception that matters the most in democracy in general but more so during electoral season, this has become now almost an insurmountable divide. Post-Sachar Committee report there is enough data to prove that Muslims are badly off in terms of education and economic opportunities, and in some cases this is worse off than even Dalits, and therefore to make special provisions for Muslims, including demanding reservations on religious grounds or including them in the OBCs is only a necessary corrective measure. When Jats and Rajputs are being included in the OBC list and Gujjars in Rajasthan are demanding to be recognised as STs, there is very little justification in denying Muslims their due share in the resources of the State. Even if the Constitution does not recognise affirmative action on religious grounds there is enough sociological reasoning behind demanding special provisions for the Muslims. Legal reasoning and pronouncements of the Court are not absolute but need to be opened up for the emerging reality because many of the legal pronouncements themselves are based on no specific logic except reinforcing the popular perceptions about justice, including the cap on reservations not crossing 50 per cent that has no special logic except for maintaining a perceived idea about merit, efficiency and equal opportunity in the system. Similarly, this skewed logic that special provisions encourages vote-bank politics has been a long-standing complaint not only with Muslims but also with regard to policies for Dalits and the OBCs. While the former is seen as minority-appeasement, the later is believed to be flaring up casteism in society. Recognising specific disabilities is not reinforcing the divide but only providing a corrective to the divide that already exists and is not created by such protective policies. Further, the idea that vote-bank politics is limited to Muslims and Dalits is itself a misconception perpetuated for way too long by the dominant social groups, both religious and caste-based. Is it not true that upper castes and upper classes vote as vote-banks in India? How else can one explain the popularity of BJP in urban areas and among caste Hindus? The dominant social- religious and caste-groups take recourse to the reasoning of individual rational choice but have voted as clusters all along.

However, the problem with the secular-communal divide does not end here. The language and discourse of secularism itself has entered an irretrievable crisis across the world. In Europe the secular separation of religion and politics was followed up by multiculturalism as preservation of cultural differences, which has only resulted in increasing ghettoisation of religious minorities and created 'parallel societies' and demands, mostly on Muslim populations, to demonstrate loyalty, and adopt 'our' values of the dominant community. This has given a fillip to not only separation of communities but also, what Slavoj Zizek refers to as, 'racism at distance'. Now Europe is exploring the possibility of shifting from multiculturalism to pluralism in order to open up inter-cultural dialogic spaces. In India too, secularism has contributed to entrenching received ideas about religious minorities, mostly Muslims. It has rarely succeeded in opening up a dialogue between religious communities. How much is known about what majority of Muslims feel about M.F. Husain painting Hindu goddesses in the nude, or about Hindus being killed in

Bangladesh or Baluchistan. There is an impending need to overcome the 'fear' of listening to their voices. Similarly, in a democracy it is only proper to expect them to respond to forms of injustice that not merely hurts them but also other vulnerable social groups. As we do not expect women alone to speak up on women's issues, or Muslims alone to speak on issues of communal violence, we cannot expect Muslims too to speak up only on issues related to religious minorities. It could, in fact be argued that Muslim groups that protest against exceptionalism of the State in Kashmir, and the witch-hunt in the name of terrorism and 'suspect Muslim', also speak up against these very methods against the tribals in Chhattisgarh, and the citizens of the northeast. Unless on some parameter religious minorities do not come across as themselves being 'secular' then the far-right forces would continue to exploit these silences for sectarian mobilisation. This is not to demand loyalty but to move beyond secular sectarianism in speaking for others. This is not a demand to prove legitimacy of 'their' belonging but a legitimate-dignifying- demand that ought to be made in any healthy democracy.

The roots of communalism are fast shifting. They no longer exist 'merely' in the memory of partition or modern day terrorism, they are in fact emerging from an entrenched caste-psyche. Caste is a ladder-like structure with every group having a dual-positionality with an oppressor above and oppressed below. Keeping caste privileges and also undoing caste for every individual sub-group is as much about unsettling those above as keeping those below in their downgraded positioning. Anti-caste movements have exclusively addressed the atrocities of those above but never as much simultaneously articulated the caste hegemony towards those below by this very same sub group/sub castes. The momentum today is much in terms of maintaining this caste hegemony and subjugating those below. Subjugating those below is the most readily available strategy to undo the humiliation—as a quick psychological relief/ empowerment—perpetuated by those above in the caste ladder. This reverse osmosis of caste groups has lead to a process of searching for and identifying groups that are relatively weak socially, politically and economically, and this process goes down all the way to the smallest and most underprivileged caste groups. This is the psyche that allows for the dominant groups to self-represent themselves as victims and the lesser privileged as enjoying undue largesse and thereby as either opportunists with regard to the Dalits or as aggressors with regard to Muslims. However, in this search for the weak, the buck seems to finally stop with identifying Muslims as the necessary 'other'. They are weaker, perceived to be 'outsiders' and perhaps the most vulnerable social group in India, combined with an imagination of the community being aggressive. The failure of the political project of building a 'Bahujan Samaj' reveals the limits of 'secular upsurge' in India. The cynicism of caste-psyche that produces the Muslim as the 'other' is ironically also the source to maintain and consolidate the Hindu fold against its internal fractures along caste lines for the Hindutva brand of mobilisation. Growing mobility for marginalised caste groups has resulted in increasing caste-conflicts and in turn widespread communal violence. Entrenched sectarianism of the caste system cannot be however tackled with secular sectarianism that dithers from asking religious minorities to address issues of justice across religious and other social identities. Strangely, the Hindutva brand of politics seems to be a step ahead in articulating the idea of 'justice for all', which should have ideally come from those championing secularism and more so from the religious minorities themselves.

Published in *The Hindu*, March 25, 2014.

9

Indian Ideology

Review of The Indian Ideology *by Perry Anderson (Three Essays Collective, Delhi, 2013).*

This book contains three essays published earlier in the *London Review of Books* in the summer of 2012. It attempts to critically engage with the nationalist discourse, and the 'ensuing hegemony of the edulcorated versions of the national past' as represented by the 'the liberal mainstream of Indian intellectual life'. The central concern is to re-contextualise the ideas of Gandhi, Nehru and Patel in the anti-colonial struggle and squarely foreground Gandhi's socially conservative frame, especially with the question of caste; Nehru's majoritarian impulse that was responsible for the partition, and Patel's uber-patriotism that sowed the seeds for the wanton use of force with impunity by the Indian State. These essays convey a sense of urgency to respond to the representative liberal scholars who have come to firmly believe in the historically unprecedented achievements of India being not just 'the world's largest democracy', but also a great one, given the conditions in which she opted for universal adult franchise, federalism, secularism, and socialism. Notwithstanding the limitations, liberal scholars, have long, projected Indian democracy as nothing short of a historical wonderland that had its roots in the inclusive, composite, cosmopolitan, socialist rhetoric of its national leaders, and the fine balance they achieved through mutually learning from each other.

It is the myth of this fine balance and the stronghold of these ideas in Indian democracy that Perry Anderson, attempts to break, through his critical insights and historical narrative, albeit all too familiar. It has all the familiar ingredients of a critical recipe, including the Poona Pact and Ambedkar's humiliation; the inconsistent position of Gandhi on the question of caste; the history of Kashmir's 'accession' to India; how Congress, and not the Muslim League, was primarily responsible for the partition in order to maintain its monopoly of power and 'saturating its appeal with a Hindu imaginary'; the role of Patel in compelling the Princely states to submit themselves in recognising the sovereign power of the Indian union; and finally the not too impressive post-independence record of Nehru, including his failure to implement land reforms, the neglect of primary education, and the policy thrust to protect the interests of rich farmers, traders and urban professionals.

While Anderson's myth-busting efforts are well taken, he has not considered previous critiques of the nationalist history, primarily, by Dalit and Marxist scholars in India. Those familiar with these writings will find very little that is new in the critique that Anderson offers, and would realise that hegemony of nationalist ideology is severely limited to certain kind of liberal-mainstream scholars and readers, beyond those horizons it is difficult to find 'The Indian Ideology', either in the Indian academia or in Indian politics. Given the sweep of Anderson's scholarship and previous engagement with Gramsci, the book would have read better had it picked on more intriguing issues that are still open to historical audition. The significant among them being the subaltern studies/postcolonial approach to Indian history that has appropriated not only Gandhi's critique of the West but also the Dalit critique of Gandhi, without ever attempting to reconcile the two. While socially conservative views of Gandhi on caste are fairly rehearsed, there are new issues that need an opening, including how the Left approaches the role and legacy of Ambedkar, whose arduous efforts, given his historical context, are laudable, his emphasis on State, and law-making, and in the end somewhat naïve emphasis on Buddhism as a way out for modern complexities, need a fresh analysis instead of the same myth-making approach that Anderson (is actually critical of) adopts towards him, and indeed to Subhas Chandra Bose. Ambedkar on the one hand was a modernist but on the other found solace in Buddhism, which, in a sense, was a scathing indictment of modern structures. This is akin to the puzzle of why Gandhi despite his critique of modernity, chose Nehru, who was a high-modernist, as his political heir. Did then, Gandhi's critique of modernity look more plausible riding on the cultural capital of Nehru? This reminds one of Sarojini Naidu's remark that it was way too expensive to keep Gandhi poor. What then was similar or dissimilar between the accommodation of modernity in Ambedkar and Gandhi? Had Anderson put his Marxist frame and Gramscian overtures into play, he would have undoubtedly been able to throw new light on some of these 'antinomies', instead of the kind of rather simplistic reasoning he presents. For instance, on the relation between Gandhi and Nehru, Anderson merely reduces it to 'calculations of mutual interest', 'quasi-filial infatuation' and 'infantilism'.

Anderson makes sense of many of the decisions and historically contingent events through a very incisive reading of the kind of individuals that some of the national leaders were, especially Nehru. He takes delight in pointing to Nehru's relations with Edwina, and Mrs. Gandhi's alleged affair with M.O. Mathai. He, insists that, many of the events, be it partition or the debacle of 1962, owed much to the inability of Nehru in judging the character of individuals around him, and also was vulnerable to self-deception, and 'drifted easily away from realities resistant to his hopes and fancies'. These might look like individual traits from a certain viewpoint—'a view from nowhere'—but if one were to politically analyse them, they could well be practices endemic to a communitarian context. Self-deception, the enduring gap between thinking and being, non-linear mode of operation, are practices through which the community finds its functional and sociological actualisation. Such inflections would be imperative for any historical rendering, where the community continues to be the basic unit of the society. What, however, comes through very convincingly in the book is the fact that making of any kind of heroes, legends and icons can only be achieved by ironing out 'self-contradictions', be they elite or even subaltern icons; as Gandhi has been sieved through history, so will Ambedkar. It is in critical engagement, as against iconoclastic rendering of nationalist heroes and the politics of patronage (reflected in uncritical glorification) practiced towards subaltern icons, that we actually and duly recognise their historical role. To that extent this book, even if partially, represents an agenda that is already well-set within the political and academic horizon of social scientists in India.

Published in *Studies in Indian Politics*, July 2013, Vol. 1.

10

Subaltern and the Post-Colonial Theory

Review of Post-Colonial Theory and the Spectre of Capital *by Vivek Chibber (Navayana, New Delhi, 2013).*

Have post-colonial theory and subaltern studies in their attempt to point towards difference, consciously or unconsciously, reproduced colonial ideology and an Orientalist description of the subaltern and her politics in India? Have they arrested the agency of the peasants and working class in assuming that modern democracy and the language of political rights was the gift of the bourgeoisie? Do they indulge in the culturalisation of the economy and politics in assuming culture as a meta-category to explain events, historical and contemporary, in Indian politics and undermine the sagacity of Capital and its capacity to universalise itself, even where pre-capitalist modes of cultural expression remain? Do they commit a category mistake in selective rendering of history in assuming that modern forms are more regulatory than the 'traditional' structures of caste, clan-based enumeration, and bio-politics of untouchability? Vivek Chibber's book is unequivocal in answering these questions in an affirmative voice and highlights these as serious theoretical and epistemic limits of post-colonial theory in general and Subaltern Studies in particular.

Many of the assumptions of the post-colonial theory borrow the Orientalist orientation, and try to explain how they make a difference to the way the subaltern politics play out. They, in other words, have all through attempted to dignify 'Orientalism', rather than invoke categories than genuinely stand outside Euro-Centrism. Could it then be possible that post-colonial theory has only offered categories that are mirror-images of Western/Enlightenment Liberalism rather than alternatives that stand outside such an 'epistemic community'? The project of Subaltern Studies, at its core, believed that workers and peasants 'lack any concept of individuality, are inured in hierarchy, and remain unmoved by calls for equality. They can erupt into orgies of violence at the slightest provocation. Their consciousness is 'split' between the modern and the traditional. And so on. (Dipesh-my addition) Chakrabarthy unloads these bromides without even a hint of self-conciousness, without any recognition of their affiliation with traditional colonial ideology...furthermore they have found an incredibly friendly audience in American academia' (p. 185-86). It is also intriguing that post-colonial theorists from India have actually flown with the stream in terms of the shift in global theoretical frames. They began as Gramscians, moved on to Heidegger, to Laclau and Mouffe, Foucault and post-structuralism, and autonomist philosophers. Their history of the subaltern in India, notwithstanding all the emphasis on difference, strangely is in alignment with the global renderings of political moves beginning with structural explanations of peasant rebellions, to discursive contests over hegemonic articulations, to more contemporary versions of post-structural politics of contingency, contextual negotiations, molecular change, politics of the possible and politics of the everyday. Indian subaltern is, ironically, local and very global at the same time.

Could these parallels have something to do with the way the agency of the subaltern has been approached within the Subaltern studies framework? Does it have something to do with their narration of European history where the 'bourgeoisie successfully integrated the popular into the domain of elite and organised politics', while 'Colonial capital's refusal to take up its universalising mission, its willingness to accommodate the ancient regime, has some important implications for political analysis' (p. 15). Vivek Chibber says, 'I will argue that the claims for a fundamental difference with regard to capital, power and agency are all irredeemably flawed...The point is not to insist that there are no differences at all between the two; rather, that the differences, such as they are, are not of the kind described by the Subalternists' (p. 23). The subaltern scholars have rarely written on the working class struggles in Europe, as much as they have written about the nature of Bourgeois capital, though one cannot be understood in the absence of the other. Did the bourgeoisie play a progressive role in Europe on its own accord or was it due to the organised struggle of the working class? This also necessitates a reasoning of the relation between capital and social identities and hierarchies. Here, capital has worked itself both ways; it could definitionally speaking work itself independent of social hierarchies, in fact that is what was unique about capitalism that it was based on a wage labour system for extraction of surplus and did not depend structurally on extra-economic force. However, functionally, capital draws from all existing social and cultural resources to augment production process and extract surplus through cheap labour and raw materials. This duality of capital is what renders history complex and in a sense, indeterminate and different. Yet, this indeterminacy occurs within the structural context of capitals drive for profits and extraction of surplus, which has the capacity to iron-out cultural differences and undermine the capacity of societies to stand outside its machinations. This fact of capital's capacity—'double movement'—allows for a global history of capitalism, with and without differences. This stands all the more true with the nature of neoliberal capital that seems to have abandoned the enlightenment project of freedom, autonomy, and dignity. It could provide women with new opportunities in the market, yet reproduce caste differences within a factory; it could intensify commodification of religion, astrology and Ayurveda, whose mere existence does not necessarily therefore signify 'Limits of Capital'. This is akin to the Subaltern theorists understanding that mere use of religious forms make Subaltern radical—without being hegemonised—and different—belong to an 'autonomous domain'—and not the nature of demands those forms are put to. Even here the attempt by the Subaltern scholars has been to dignify the practices of the subaltern as they exist, rather than account for how agency is determined by the way power is structured and resources constrain choice of political action. While, in highly prejudiced social and communitarian context this might hold some value, it also for this very reason suffers from reifying the modern and 'ethnicisation of the subaltern'.

Subaltern Studies project has claimed a kind of autonomy for culture that is in some sense supra-historical. It has understood capital through culture and culture in its difference with enlightenment. In this mode of analysis it has opted for a selective rendering of history and politics. While one way to make sense is that in itself it was a political project of its times, and therefore historically constrained to forge a narrative that is entrenched in its singular focus on drawing a binary opposition with Western enlightenment. However, the political fallout of such a selective rendering has been severely limited in imagining alternative modes of political articulation. This could be pursued, for instance, not merely in highlighting the difference but also the alignment and layered nature of social and cultural practices. Colonial rule was to a large extent based on the already existing social hierarchies, which were neither created nor institutionalised by the colonial state. Governmentality is no more regulating than the already existing systems of enumeration based on clan that was integral to the way caste was reproduced. Similarly, practices of untouchability were deeply bio-political and techniques of disciplining that did not originate with modern forms of power. It could well be the case that modern forms of power draw on the already existing modes of culture, including that of the subaltern. However, much of post-colonial theory has very selectively only foregrounded the 'creative power of community' without ever laying out the practices internal to the formation of such collectives. The fantasy of community, as Zygmunt Bauman would put it, has haunted the post-colonial project as an 'empty category' that is necessarily only made sense of as the other of modernity. Post-colonial theorists have held on to this 'fantasy' even as they have increasingly grown critical of utopias of the Left/Marxist variant.

It is however, interesting to observe that Vivek's book has been published just when Partha Chatterjee has written an obituary of the Subaltern project. His more recent understanding has been driven by what he argues is the governmentalisation of subaltern subjectivity, and their contemporary politics is all about negotiating for subsistence benefits within what he refers to as the 'political society'. It would have been even more valuable had Vivek had the opportunity to take these new developments into account. Notwithstanding that, this remains an important contribution in the emerging literature that critically engages with post-colonial theory, and might contribute significantly to move beyond entrenched post-colonial theory towards more open-ended transnational possibilities.

Published in the *Book Review*.

Small States and Formation of Telangana

11

The State of Popular Aspiration

With the United Progressive Alliance (UPA) constituting a committee on Telangana, it shall definitely assume significant proportions in this winter session of Parliament. One has to wait and see if the issue moves beyond constituting the second States' Reorganisation Committee (SRC) and there are efforts to actually carve out an independent state of Telangana. A lot depends not only on how effectively the leaders of Telangana Rashtra Samithi (TRS) would plead and convince, and also at times threaten, since it is not very long ago that TRS leader Chandrasekhar threatened to 'drag Sonia Gandhi onto the streets, if demand for a separate Telangana is not fulfilled'. There is a need to convince the 'High Command' and the Left parties as their opposition is well known and was the reason why despite the alliance, the TRS put up its candidates at many places in the recent Assembly elections in AP.

It is perhaps important to note that the Andhra BJP has taken a pro-Telangana stand. BJP has a stronger support base in Telangana than in coastal Andhra. Undoubtedly BJP stands to gain with the formation of a separate state, and it is only due to the compulsions of alliance politics (with the TDP) that it underplayed the issue.

The issue of separate statehood to Telengana is by no means new. The first States' Reorganisation Committee in the early 1950s, much before it has been an electoral issue, recognised it. However, in applying and implementing the States' Reorganisation Act, 1955, the Central Government developed four formal rules:

- No reorganisation for groups that made secessionist demands (for states like Sikkim);
- No accommodation of regional demands based on religious grounds (in light of the problem of Punjab);
- No linguistic recognition unless out of popular demand (in 1954, for instance, Western Uttar Pradesh wanted a separate state but was not a popular mass demand);
- No reorganisation if the demand came from only one of the important language groups (for instance, with the Madras province both the Telugu and Tamil-speaking people wanted a reorganisation).

Apart from the fact that the first SRC cautioned against reorganisation solely on linguistic grounds, the demand for Telangana fulfils the entire criterion including the last one. Contrary to popular perceptions, common people in coastal Andhra are not quite opposed to the idea of a separate Telangana state. It was more than evident in the recent Assembly elections where despite the TDP raking up Telugu pride and Andhra sentiment by suggesting a possible water crisis due to sharing of river water, it could not garner a substantial percentage of vote or seats in the coastal districts.

Telengana is the largest region of the state, with a population and area that is more than that of both coastal Andhra and the Rayalseema, covering 41.47% of the state area and 40.54% of the total inhabitants. It, in fact contributes more than 50% to the state revenue.Inspite of this Telangana was denied a rightful share in river water by successive governments. Many of the districts are suffering from acute water crisis and some like Mahabubnagar have become drought prone. All major irrigation projects are undertaken to benefit the coastal regions where irrigation with canal system is up to 74.25%, while farmers in Telangana are forced to pay for digging bore wells and pay heavy electricity charges on using them. With bores drying up due to low underground water levels, agriculture has become increasingly untenable leading to a spate of farmers' suicides very recently (apart from the handloom workers suicides).

The literacy rate in Telangana is even today less than 50%. It is because the share of Telangana is less than 20% in the total quantum of grant-in-aid (Department of Higher Education, AP). Culturally, the Telangana dialect is looked down upon and the Telugu film industry, which is dominated by producers who were rich farmers and has its lead roles played by actors also from the coastal regions while representing people from Telangana as the stereotypical villain. The coastal rich also dominate the print and electronic media.

However, the real question is whether the formation of a separate and smaller state would really address Telangana's problems? If so, would the common people be the real beneficiaries, or would benefits go to a minute privileged section that already wields economic power? The latter comprise of landed castes with active support from the NRIs belonging to the Telangana region who are now in search of political power? Individuals and organisations championing the cause of Telangana need to raise the following issues: patterns of land ownership and accompanying caste-class dynamics. The implementation of minimum wages. Free primary education for all below the age of 14 years with schemes such as the mid-day meal and providing qualified teachers and necessary infrastructure. Restricting privatisation and corporatisation of the health sector and compel them to follow mandatory free service to the people from poorer sections. Continuation of various welfare policies including subsidisation of agriculture (such as free electricity). Monitoring both fluctuating prices and selling of spurious seeds. Generating employment and social security measures for the workers in the growing unorganised sector. Rehabilitating the urban poor such as those displaced migrant labour, which migrated to Hyderabad city mostly as daily wage labourers and construction workers. Reactivating Pollution Control Boards against industries (mostly in the new industrial towns that have emerged around the capital city in the Ranga Reddy district). Letting out untreated affluent into tanks built for drinking water which have led to grave health disorders. Arresting rampant urbanisation which has led to a severe drinking water crisis along with traffic-related pollution and steep rise in real estate making housing unaffordable to lower income groups.

The current leadership of Telangana does not seem to raise

or possess a clear perspective on any of these issues, which is what makes the demand for Telangana hollow, as such a demand could then end up serving the aspirations of the privileged class. The struggle for Telangana is a struggle for ordinary people to find a geographical entity that would better their lives.Without a commitment to those ordinary people, achieving Telangana would simply be a betrayal of the aspirations of a large section of deprived groups. Telangana is therefore a rather poignantly paradoxical conjecture where the demand is democratic but realising it might not be.

Published in *The Indian Express*, February 5, 2005.

12

Tangles of Telangana

The sudden spate of developments in the Telangana issue reflect, more than a concern for the backwardness of Telangana, an attempt on the part of both the TDP and the Congress to make sure they do not stand to lose in either region if Telangana is granted statehood. The Congress, of course, has the additional burden of ensuring it continues to rule in both regions. Amid these calculations, the core demands and the likelihood of their fulfilment have been pushed into the background. We need to revisit these issues if Telangana is to be something more than merely another geographical entity.

Popular aspirations in Telangana have to be understood in the context of a growing agrarian crisis, due to a shortage of irrigation facilities and increasing investment costs from the consequent dependence on private bore-wells. Together with higher power prices, this has pushed farmers to the wall—in some cases, burning their own crops when market prices were not commensurate with input costs. Currently, 77 per cent of irrigation in Telangana is from bore-wells and open wells, while in coastal Andhra 58 per cent is through canals built through public investment.

Similarly, people of occupational or service castes—potters, blacksmiths and goldsmiths—have lost their traditional forms of livelihood, partly because of the impact of larger businesses. Today, many "joint action committees" have been created in each district by organisations belonging to various service castes. They, in a sense, are the "invisible" backbone of the movement, while students are the more visible leaders, apart from Dalits and Muslim organisations. These committees are only partially controlled by political parties, and to a large extent are a spontaneous response, managed through resources raised voluntarily and locally. They all strongly believe a new state is the only way to better living conditions.

While the democratic aspirations of the people need to be addressed, we also need to ask how these groups will be accommodated in the new state of Telangana. While OBCs, Dalits, Muslims and students are the driving force of the movement, there is unfortunately very little in the content of the movement to concretely fulfil their demands. For example, while there is hope that the division of water resources will be fairer, and the water from Krishna and Godavari rivers will be directed to the districts of Telangana, there is no commensurate demand for land reforms on any notable scale. Water without land is beneficial to a small section of the agrarian class and promises nothing for the large number of landless labourers who routinely migrate to other states. Among India's highest rates of out-migration is from the district of Mahbubnangar.

The BJP's support to Telangana has been strong; the bill cannot be passed in Parliament without its support. The party argues that, in principle, it supports smaller states, crediting itself with the formation of Chhattisgarh, Uttarakhand and Jharkhand. In fact, the BJP sees Telangana as its second stop in the south, after Karnataka. Most districts in Telangana have a sizeable Muslim population, between 10 and 14 per cent. Many continue to pride themselves on the fact that they were once the rulers of this region. The combination of a large population and a memory of a glorious past can be a potent combination for communal mobilisation and polarisation. Recall that the city of Hyderabad has been prone to communal riots, and there is very little reason as to why the BJP will not play this card again in the smaller state of Telangana with a more visible and concentrated Muslim population.

The next issue of concern is the plight of a large number of settlers from coastal Andhra—mostly in Hyderabad, but also in other districts. There is a good-sized population of "migrants", mostly small traders and semi-skilled workers. Credit must be given to the Telangana movement that there has been, so far, no popular sentiment against ordinary people from the Andhra region, which is largely directed at those considered "responsible" for deliberate mismanagement and exploitation, including political and business leaders.

However, as of now, there is little possibility of a large number of jobs being created in the new state of Telangana. People are not aspiring, for example, for a clear programme that creates labour-intensive industries. Nor is there any possibility of a great number of public-sector jobs except for those created with a small (maybe a few thousand) government employees being moved or transferred to the Andhra region. Continuing unemployment will have a definite impact on the students who have sustained the movement in expectation of moving up the social and economic ladder — which in turn might act against the "settlers" from the Andhra region.

These tangled issues need to raised today if there has to be a democratic Telangana, in whose name the struggle has gathered immense momentum, otherwise there will be none to blame tomorrow, not even the "capitalists" from the Andhra region.

Published in *The Indian Express*, July 11, 2011.

13

Telangana: Nation, State and the City

The Congress after hastily announcing the initiation of the process of formation of a separate state of Telangana on December 9, 2009, has been procrastinating on the final decision, as only the Congress could do. Part of the reason for this is that Congress continues to look for a win-win strategy in both the regions—Telangana and coastal Andhra, and it could not find one, in all these years. It has now realised that it has reached a "lose-lose" situation, in both the regions of Andhra Pradesh. The single most important reason for Congress for at-least revisiting the issue is the realisation that in spite of holding up the issue of formation of a separate Telangana, it has steadily lost its popular base in the districts of coastal Andhra, which has instead shifted, in a rather dramatic manner to the newly formed YSR-Congress.

As for Telangana, it had already yielded the political space to the Telangana Rashtra Samithi (TRS), and now there is the additional predicament with the possibility of the rise of the Bharatiya Janata Party, especially after they won in Mahabubnagar district, in the recent by-elections held in March 2012. The Congress was therefore staring at a rather bleak future in both the regions of the state, which had contributed the largest number of MPs, in the previous general elections. The leadership of the Congress now realises that it cannot possibly imagine coming anywhere close to regaining power at the centre, without returning a sizeable number of MPs from Andhra Pradesh. As part of the new calculations for the forthcoming general elections, the party seems to be counting on the decision to grant a separate Telangana, as one of its electoral strategy, alongside implementing popular schemes such as direct cash transfers. This visible pressure on the Congress to take a favourable decision then needs to be attributed as much to the people of the Andhra region, as for the unrelenting struggle of those in the Telangana region.

The realisation that Telangana did not figure so significantly in the calculations of the electorate in the coastal districts, in a sense, will be the game changer. Instead, it is the welfare schemes under the YSR regime, and continuation of those that seem to matter more. However, the extensive welfare schemes imagined and implemented by the former chief minister, Y.S. Rajasekhara Reddy (YSR), have come to be seen, more as part of the political repertoire of his projected benevolent personality, rather than any sustained policy direction of the Congress Party itself. While, the high command might be ruing this popularity of YSR, and made attempts to even bury that legacy by naming him in the FIR filed in disproportionate assets against his family, including his son Jagan Mohan Reddy, who has been languishing in the jail for close to a year now. Jagan Mohan Reddy, in effect, has been reaping the benefits of the extensive welfare programmes that were almost meticulously implemented by YSR. While, one might have aversion to dynasty politics, it needs to however be understood in the context of the neoliberal reforms. With neoliberalism, and the advent of global capital, and global market mechanisms, governments look helpless in controlling price rise, and in disbursing subsidies. There is a sense of facelessness to this process that has also made it difficult distinguishing the policy frame of one political party from the other. In such an eventuality, individual personalities, families become tangible targets on whom onus can be laid. They become symbols, who are either acknowledged or rejected, in the face of the kind of contingency that electorates experience in receiving even minimal benefits, and social security measures reaching them. The shift from party to personality in coastal Andhra got coupled with the shift from party to region, in Telangana. There was, in fact, a suggestion for the formation of a separate political outfit—the Telangana Democratic Front, with all the MPs and MLAs, from all the political parties in the Telangana region, joining together. The new imagination around popular support, right from the beginning of this struggle for a separate Telangana, cut across party affiliations. Between personality-cult and regional aspirations, the Congress had lost much of its political relevance.

Developments in Coastal Andhra and Rayalseema

Had the Congress managed to maintain some popular support base in coastal Andhra, it could have been a very different story all together. The Congress did attempt to turn it around in coastal Andhra by launching Chiranjeevi, with the merger of his party Praja Rajyam into the Congress, as its leader. However, he failed to capture the popular imagination and that experiment was a non-starter. The situation gained further clarity with Jagan Mohan Reddy not being allowed to carry out his *odarpu yatra* in the Telangana region, since he was seen as voice for united Andhra Pradesh. His entourage was attacked by students in Warangal; he had to beat a hasty retreat, and never campaigned in the Telangana region. It was also clear that YSR himself did not enjoy the kind of credibility and mass following in the Telangana region that he had in Seemandhra. Part of the reason for YSR's unpopularity was the fact that agrarian crisis in the Telangana region became more acute during his time, and he launched new projects such as *Polavaram*, to procure more water resources to the Andhra region, and kept those under-construction projects in the Telangana region that were supposed procure water for the Telangana region, in abeyance. It is an irony that while the struggle for a separate Telangana began due to the agrarian crisis, it has entered a stalemate around the question of Hyderabad. Akin to the shift of focus from land reforms to land acquisition in the last three decades, the contentious issue in the formation of a separate Telangana was the city of Hyderabad, and urban lands, in which coastal Andhra traders have massive investments. Lagdapati Rajgopal, a Congress MP from coastal Andhra, who has spearheaded the campaign (read lobbying) for a united Andhra Pradesh, himself is alleged to have had huge investments and business interests in keeping the state united. The issue thereby assumed the classical dimension of a contest between accumulation and legitimacy. In fact, the *Jai Andhra movement* in the coastal districts clearly separated themselves from these neo-rich, and argued that a separate state for Andhra people would create new investment and employment opportunities for the common people. The neo-rich from coastal Andhra made their money initially through investment of the agrarian surplus in the film and hotel industry, and more recently through speculative land dealings, real estate, irrigation and mining contracts.

The nature of the capital, and the speculative deals never created wider economic opportunities for the common people in the coastal Andhra districts. What would make a real difference with the formation of the separate state is a share in the water resources. Telangana, contrary to the popular belief, is one of the most water rich areas in the country, and has been systematically deprived of these resources as a fall-out of conscious state-policy, due to which it suffered from acute agrarian crisis, leading up to a spate of farmers' suicides. Within this unfolding drama, the third region of Rayalseema has become the theatre of the absurd. While all important leaders in the AP politics today, including Chandrababu Naidu, the chief of the Telugu Desam Party, Jagan Mohan Reddy of YSR-Congress, and the Kiran Kumar Reddy, the current chief minister of AP, belong to the Rayalseema region, it has still remained neglected. Rayalseema being an arid region has remained economically backward, and culturally fraught with factionalism. Thus, while the economic capital belonged to the coastal regions, the political power was handled by those from the Rayalseema; in that sense it did not suffer from deep-rooted feeling of being neglected. People from the Telangana region had neither. Added to that was a conscious policy of abject neglect of Telangana, which was treated like a colonial hinterland, and culturally denigrated.

The political developments in the eventuality of the formation of a separate state of Telangana are many. The TRS was all along a party with a single agenda of fighting for separate statehood, beyond which it has no social or political vision. The popularity of the party and its leadership is inextricably tied to the demand itself. It would therefore be not much of a surprise if the TRS decides to merge in Congress, in order to extend its political innings.

In fact, its chief, K. Chandrasekahar Rao (popularly called KCR), has already, for some time now, made an image-makeover from his aggressive posturing in the past to a statesman-like behaviour; though he has announced in the past that the first chief minister of the separate state would be a dalit. As for the TDP, it has already lost many of its top leaders who quit the party to either remain independent, or join the TRS. Whether or not TDP will continue to be a relevant political force in the separate state would depend on whether or not it manages to keep its traditional social base among the OBCs. This question becomes all the more precarious with the rise of the BJP, which has the potential to knock-off this base from them. This also leads us to the question of the Muslims, who constitute 10-14% in most of the 10 districts of the Telangana region. This is also the reason why the BJP visualises Telangana as its second-stop in the south, after Karnataka. As I had pointed out elsewhere, the memory of once having belonged to the ruling elite among the Muslims combined with a sizeable population is a potent mix on which BJP can begin its anti-Muslim rhetoric.[i] Some of the events in the recent past, including the riots in Adilabad, and the recent statements and controversy surrounding the Owaisi clan (of the All India Majlis-e-Ittehadul Muslimeen) are pointers in that direction, apart from the contentious issues of a small-temple like structure that suddenly came up attached to a pillar of the adorable Charminar. These issues would in the coming days provide the required fodder for communal polarisation. It should be mentioned here that there is already, though a silent apprehension, among the caste Hindus in the Telangana region that once Telangana is achieved there would be a possibility of going back to the days of Nizam, ,meaning to the days to "Muslim domination". As for, the larger fall-out at the national level, there could be more demands for separate state including those in Gorkhaland, and Vidharba. Very much like Telangana, they are born from demands for more economic development, and better living conditions. This necessitates the government in the centre to seriously consider the possibility of constituting the second State Reorganisation Commission. Though one needs to keep in mind that more smaller states does not necessarily mean a stronger federal set-up, instead it could also mean a stronger centre.

Finally, though the movement for a separate Telangana has been waged relentlessly, and with unprecedented mobilisation in villages and districts, the national media— in whose self-imagination they are the true torchbearers for the nation— both print and electronic— have unequivocally blocked out any news on this. This is intriguing to say the least. While there are wide speculations in Telangana that the neo-rich from coastal Andhra either have direct investments in the news channels, or have bribed them, it is more likely that an issue that is not run by urban India does not interest the media. It does not make for good TV. It did not have spokespersons, unlike Koodankulam or the campaign lead by Anna Hazare, who spoke the language that the media personnel understood. It did not have urban symbolism but spoke in terms of local folklore and festivals that speak a different idiom, and carry different caste-class equations. It was primarily agrarian and rural, and if anything politicised the city and the metropolitan that were otherwise imagined to be sanitised spaces of urban recreation. Though the movement for a large part was spearheaded by the youth-young India—but unfortunately this was not "the youth" that anchors had in mind, and of course they did not speak chaste-English nor were they amenable to the patronage they wished to extend to the "vernacular". The national media has singularly played a very regressive role, and the democratic content of their anchor`s worldview stops short of substance. However, Telangana will continue to be an issue and nothing short of separate statehood will be acceptable to the people of this region. The electoral calculations of the Congress too now cannot afford to ignore the popular aspiration.

Published in the *Economic and Political Weekly*
(Web Exclusives) Vol. XLVIII, No. 5, February 2, 2013.

14

Small States, Big Problems

Smaller states have been the new political mode of addressing basic issues that were otherwise left unresolved. However, fighting for a new state and reconstructing on a more sustainable democratic content are undoubtedly two different issues all together. One does not automatically promise the other, if there is anything to learn from the previous history of smaller states in India.

The premise of carving out smaller states in India shifted from the formation of linguistic states to one of, since the 1990s, rearranging them on the basis of backwardness and a lack of development. However, even a cursory look at how Uttarakhand, Chhattisgarh and Jharkhand have fared will tell us how the mere formation of a smaller state is no guarantee for better lives for those social groups for whom these states have been created. Uttarakhand continues to be at the lower end in the Human Development Index. There was abject callousness in dealing with the recent floods, focussing solely on how to make it more tourist-friendly rather than planning for the rehabilitation of displaced residents. There was little concern demonstrated for the "local" people in whose name the State was created.

Chhattisgarh has witnessed the largest displacement of tribals in recent times. There have been sustained attempts to dispossess them of their land which they have inhabited for centuries in order to extract mineral wealth. Even as tribals were ostensibly empowered by the Panchayats (Extension to the Scheduled Areas) Act (PESA), there were attempts to invoke the clause of Eminent Domain, in the name of national interest.

The displacement of tribals was in fact "outsourced" by the state to vigilante groups formed through what was depicted as a spontaneous uprising called "Salwa Judum"—in effect an organised effort by non-tribals and traders from outside the State. How did they get the better of the tribals in whose name the State was created? Jharkhand turned out to be perhaps the worst of the three. With hardly any agenda of development worth mentioning, the State turned into a mining hell of "predatory growth," eventually resulting in a series of scams and criminal proceedings being initiated against the first tribal Chief Minister of the State. Thus, how optimistic can one get about Telangana?

Questionable Model of Growth

When states remain backward for long, they are ushered in to create new growth in order to catch up with the rest. While this kind of growth-centric discourse has been the rhetoric of the neo-liberal economy for the last three decades, it neatly overlaps with the aspirations that lie behind the creation of smaller states. However, the nature of the economy in these states remains distinct, since they are latecomers. The lack of industry, an agrarian crisis and a low level of infrastructural facilities push such states into adopting a model of development where growth can be achieved in spite of these handicaps. This, as we witnessed with the examples of the three smaller states, results in an unprecedented exploitation of raw materials such as the mining of minerals instead of the creation of industry, wanton land deals, a boost to the construction industry and the conversion of fertile agricultural land into speculative real estate transactions, since agriculture in any case was untenable and non-profitable.

Alongside these possibilities, Telangana has also been a haven for liquor contractors since a large chunk of state revenue is from liquor contracts. Civil, liquor and mining contractors have come to constitute the dominant, economic elite and the political class. Added to this speculative nature of the economy —especially in the case of Telangana—is the excessive concentration of resources in the capital city of Hyderabad. Since Hyderabad is already well-developed in terms of infrastructure, there remains little possibility of developing other smaller towns for the purpose of economic investments. It is precisely for this reason that the clamour over Hyderabad is detrimental to the interests of other backward districts in the region. Therefore, it is reasonable to bring into question how such a model of growth will be able to address the aspirations of the various social groups that have mobilised themselves relentlessly in a struggle for a separate state of Telangana. Will this model be able to address the impending agrarian crisis that has resulted in scores of farmer suicides? Will it provide employment to the students who formed the backbone of the movement? Will it provide relief to artisans and other nascent non-farm sectors in the rural hinterland? Finally, will it be able to create new avenues to stop massive migration that many districts of Telangana have witnessed in the last three decades?

Politics of Polarisation

On the political front too there are many challenges that Telangana will have to face, and this dream of a "New Telangana" that was ushered in by the leaders needs closer introspection—something that has been missing so far from the discourse. With a clear possibility of an alliance, after Telangana Rashtra Samithi (TRS) leader K. Chandrasekhar Rao rejected the idea of a merger between the TRS and the Congress, there will be no regional alternative left in the State except for the Telugu Desam Party (TDP) that has not done well electorally in the last decade or so. This will undoubtedly open up new space for the Bharatiya Janata Party (BJP) that has also championed the cause of Telangana.

Telangana was ruled by the Nizam, and most of the districts have a Muslim population not less than 13-14 per cent. Added to this is the imagination among the Muslim population that they once upon a time in history belonged to the ruling elite. It is this imagination that is always invoked by the likes of All India Majlis Ittehadul Muslimeen (MIM) chief Asaduddin Owaisi and his brother, Akbaruddin Owaisi. While as rhetoric it might provide a sense of security for the Muslims, it also creates fertile ground for the agenda of Hindutva and a politics of polarising Hindus and Muslims along religious lines. In fact, the BJP sees Telangana as its second stop in South India, after Karnataka. While the dominant castes of Reddys and Velamas constitute the leadership of the TRS and the Congress, there is a distinct possibility of the BJP shifting ground to mobilise the Other Backward Classes, weaning them away from the TDP. Along with the conservative Brahminical social elite, OBCs and even Dalits could be the social base of the BJP to pursue its Hindutva dream, leaving Telangana with no democratic social force that could counter its divisive agenda.

The sentiment of being deprived in a backward region and culturally subjugated and victimised are grounds for the demand for a separate state that can very easily be mobilised, once a new state is formed, against imagined aggressors within the state. It is for this reason that the MIM has been opposed to the demand for a separate State—an issue that was put on the back burner by the leaders championing the cause of Telangana, never looking for ways of addressing it.

In fact, when Mr. Chandrasekhar Rao once recalled the legacy of the Nizam, which was in any case problematic, it led to massive disapproval. The history of the Telangana struggle of the 1940s and the popular memory of the atrocities committed by the Razakars, the private army unleashed by the Nizam, continue to haunt public and political debate in the region, conveniently forgetting that the landlords who sided with the Razakars belonged to the now dominant Reddy and Velama castes. Much of the public campaign of the BJP in the region, alongside the demand for Telangana, was fashioned around this selective construction of history. Another Muzaffarnagar or a Gujarat cannot be ruled out in the near future in the "New" Telangana.

Published in *The Hindu*, March 14, 2014.

15

Muslims of Telangana: A Ground Report

Muslims constitute 12.5% in Telangana according to the 2001 census (Rao: 2014). However, the question that has gained prominence with the formation of Telangana is whether or not their social, political and economic position would improve, or will it further decline? Several other questions need to be looked into as well. What is the perception of Muslims about Telangana and their own future in this new state? Did they actively participate in the ten-year long struggle for a separate Telangana, or were they indifferent or even opposed to it? If so, which were the sections among the Muslims that opposed the statehood and why? Is Telangana prone to communal polarisation or has it in course of this movement become more secular and identifies with its composite culture that is often referred to as the *Ganga-Jamuni tehjeeb*? Does the idea of *samajika Telangana* subsume the significance that needs to be accorded to this section of the population, or has it neglected the question of Muslims, ignored the possibility of communal polarisation in course of its mobilisation and thereby, willy-nilly, contributed to the age-old anxiety among the Hindu population that continues to suffer with the perception of Muslim 'dominance' during the Nizam rule?

To address some of these questions, a survey was carried out by the author with the assistance of a Hyderabad-based research institute, People's Pulse, in March 2014 in three districts of Telangana that included Mahbubnagar, Nalgonda and Warangal. Purposive sampling method was used, and intense discussions were carried out with a cross-section of the Muslim community. This included leaders of various Muslim organisations such as Andhra Pradesh Muslim Empowerment Forum, ideologues of political parties such as Majlis Ittehadul Muslimeen (MIM), professional middle classes such as lawyers and doctors, journalists with Urdu and Telugu dailies, businessmen, lower middle classes such as school teachers, those pursuing informal employment and self-employed youth and Muslims that constitute the urban poor. The chairman of the Telangana Joint Action Committee (TJAC) that led the movement for a separate statehood M. Kodandram was also interviewed. Though the survey essentially focused on Muslims, a few Hindus were also interviewed.

The survey found that there is a clear polarisation between the Muslims and the Hindus in Telangana. The polarisation has in fact become sharper with the formation of a separate state because of the sizeable and concentrated population of the Muslims. The new aspirations of the Muslims for socio-economic benefits and political representation is being viewed by the dominant community as "aggressive" re-assertion by the Muslims, who were otherwise dormant and subdued in the integrated state of Andhra Pradesh.

Issue of Political Representation

The crux of the problem begins with an intriguing issue of political representation that Muslims see as an immediate panacea for many of the problems plaguing their community, while Hindus perceive this to be an undue assertion and as communalisation of the electoral processes taking "advantage" of their minority status.

The entire argument for Muslim representation is based on the premise that Muslims should get tickets from political parties in constituencies where their population is in a sizeable number, for instance in Bodhan in Nizamabad district where they constitute 39% or Mahabubnagar where they make for about 20% of the electorate. The argument being that Muslims should and rather would vote en bloc for a Muslim candidate making his/her candidature viable and bring-in a winnability factor to their candidature. This Muslims perceive is a legitimate way for them to gain political representation when they are in a numerical minority.

However, this strategy of en bloc voting is perceived by the majority community as "vote-bank" politics and communal polarisation initiated by the minority community. Hindus that we have interviewed in course of our survey, therefore, have argued that "if Muslims can vote en bloc for a Muslim candidate, then what is wrong in Hindus voting en bloc for a Hindu candidate", (that too cutting across caste-lines which is considered to be a "progressive" move and further complicates the issue). The counter-argument to this by the Muslims is that Muslims are willing to vote for all political parties (except the Bharatiya Janata Party [BJP]) when they offer tickets to Hindu candidates, but Hindus are unwilling to vote for Muslim candidates, irrespective of the political party that offers them the ticket.

2009 Assembly Elections

It is this stalemate that has been witnessed in course of the decade-long political movement for the formation of a separate state. In Mahabubnagar district in 2009 Assembly elections, Rajeshwar Reddy, who was active with the BJP, contested as an independent candidate, as the BJP offered a ticket to Padmaja Reddy, while the Telangana Rashtra Samiti (TRS) offered a ticket to Ibrahim. Rajeshwar Reddy won the elections; he however passed away in 2010, leading to by-elections in 2011. After which, the Congress offered a ticket to an Other Backward Classes (OBC) candidate Muthyala Prakash, while the TRS offered it to Ibrahim and BJP's candidate was N.M. Srinivas Reddy.

These elections witnessed a sharp polarisation of votes against Ibrahim and consolidation of Hindu votes for the BJP candidate Srinivas Reddy. The BJP not only campaigned for a separate state of Telangana but also against the "re-assertion designs" of the minority community. The BJP`s Member of Parliament (MP) Hema Malini came to campaign here and argued that "what we are witnessing in these elections is a India-Pakistan Match, now you decide whether you wish to support India or Pakistan"; Pakistan being a veiled reference to the TRS candidate Ibrahim.[2]

Public processions resorted to slogans such as *"Ek do ek do Muslim ko Phek do"*(one two, one two, chuck the Muslim). Some of the Muslims we interviewed recollected an incident where *"Ma ko Bachao"* (save the mother) was painted on a stray cow, which was let loose in the streets. This was again a campaign against beef eating by Muslims. Prior to this, some of the Muslim respondents recollected an incident where in the nearby Hanuman Mandir some unknown people beheaded the statue of Hanuman. Muslims suspect that this was done by Hindus themselves, belonging to the BJP or the RSS, in order to escalate the tensions between both the communities. As a result, the BJP candidate Srinivas Reddy won with an overwhelming majority.

Muslims pointed out that in the by-election for 11seats, which was the high point in the agitation for a separate state, the TRS won 10 seats and the only seat it lost was that of a Muslim candidate. One of our respondent Abdullah, a school teacher, pointed out that even the TJAC, which is otherwise secular, campaigned here for the BJP candidate. The TJAC has its own reasoning that it was important to take the BJP on board since their support was indispensable if the Telangana Bill was to be passed in the Parliament.[3]

Going Back in History

The defeat of Ibrahim has been resonating across Telangana. In all three districts, Muslim respondents referred to this issue, which is of singular importance in understanding how the electorate is getting polarised across religious lines. However, it is important to understand that this process is historical in nature going back all the way to the fact that Telangana, which was a part of the Hyderabad State, was ruled by the Nizam (Gudavarthy: 2014). His rule ended with a bitter conflict that resulted in "Police Action", in which it is widely believed that about 2-3 lakh Muslims were killed and atrocities were committed by the private militia of the Nizam *the Razakars*. In fact, "The Andhra Pradesh unit of the BJP called upon people of Telangana and political parties there to celebrate 17th September as 'Telangana Liberation Day' to commemorate the region's freedom from erstwhile Nizam rule". (*The Hindu*: 2011)

Muslims feel that they belonged to the ruling elite, and that the Nizam was a secular ruler who gave land to the Hindus and made them *Deshmukhs* and started a great number of institutions such as the Osmania University, Osmania General Hospital, among others.[4] However, he continues to be vilified as a despot. Muslims would argue that all kings were feudal in nature, but then while the legacy of Hindu kings is positively appropriated and preserved, the Nizam alone is vilified for being feudal. This is squarely because he was a Muslim ruler.

The aftermath of the ousting of the Nizam has witnessed a drastic decline in the social, political and economic position of the Muslims. Urdu was removed as an official language, which made the modern education unavailable for the Muslims. Their percentage came down from 40% in government jobs in 1950 to about 5% in 2010. They earlier owned land to the tune of 35% but now it is less than 4%, after they were displaced from the villages in the course of the "Police Action", and these lands have been taken over by the Reddys and Velemas. Therefore, at the heart of the conflict with Muslims is also the struggle about economic power that was wrested from them by the castes that are now dominant.

Better Opportunities or Futher Marginalisation?

Now about 70% of Muslims reside mostly in small towns and cities and are employed as mechanics, artisans, auto and bus drivers, plumbers, tailors, running road side tea stalls, while others with government jobs are mostly school teachers or police constables. Since they do not own land, and the Telangana movement was essentially about land and water and agrarian crisis, its agenda did not directly appeal to Muslims. Hasan Kalim, a school teacher in Nalgonda district sums up this despondency when he says "*Aandha ko din kya raath kya, ek hi baath ha*", (For a blind man whether it is day or night, it is the same thing); the plight of Muslims in Telangana is just that. The creation of a new state will not make any difference, as they are far too backward and socially marginalised to benefit from a smaller state.

Subhan, an insurance agent in Mahbubnagar pointed out

that "Hindus do not have dignity of labour, if they are educated they remain unemployed and do not work, but even a post-graduate Muslim will drive an auto or work as a mechanic to eek out a living". In contrast, Hari, a young lawyer pointed out that "since Muslims fend for themselves, they have to be aggressive to survive, and therefore they become very dominating and also courageous".[5]

Hindu's believe that after Urdu was removed as the official language Muslims never tried to "integrate" with the rest of the society and never studied in Telugu or in English, and that is the reason they lost out on government jobs, and not because they were ever explicitly discriminated against. Many Hindu respondents argued, "what prevented them from coming out of Madrasa education and adopt modern education. Why are they so prejudiced against Telugu language"? It is this unwillingness on the part of the Muslims that many argue is what makes the majority community suspicious of them. They further believe that Telugu was neglected as a language under the Nizam.

Muslim participation for a separate state oscillated between silent and dormant support among those in villages, to indifference among those pursuing semi-skilled jobs in the towns, to enthusiasm among middle class Muslims in professions such as lawyers and doctors and university and college teachers to opposition by those residing in Hyderabad and those who support the MIM in districts. The popular perception among the Hindus again oscillates between angst that Muslims did not actively support the movement (one of the Hindu respondent Gopal Krishna in fact asked "Did even a single Muslim lose his or her life for Telangana?"), and the possibility that once Telangana is realised, since they are concentrated, they would assert and "dream" about return to the "old times".[6]

Muslims on the other hand fear that with the creation of the state of Telangana they become more vulnerable, as there is a distinct possibility of the growth of right-wing forces, including the Vishwa Hindu Parishad (VHP), the RSS and the BJP.

Communal Polarisation

It is partly true that many of the Muslims, especially those who are politically active do take pride in the leadership of the Nizam, and the fact that he once patronised the Hindus. Md Abdul Hazim, district president of the MIM in Mahabubnagar, argued that "while Nizam gave lands to Hindus, in their rule they want to send us back to either Pakistan or *Kabrastan* (grave yard)". He further added, the Hindu rulers give us "either *gali or goli* (abuse or the bullet)". He also observed that Hindus had no choice but to choose India as their nation during partition, while Muslims had a choice and yet decided to stay back in Hindustan. "Now who is more patriotic?", he asked.

Anees Muqthadar, president of the AP Muslim Empowerment Forum in Nalgonda district, made an interesting observation that while the Andhra region has regionalism, Telangana has communalism. While in the Andhra region Muslims are referred to as *"sahebl"*, in Telengana they are derogatively referred to as *"Turkollu"* (those who came from Turkey). Economic development in Andhra region has integrated Muslims, and backwardness in Telangana has led to their wide-scale marginalisation.

Anees pointed out that in 2009 assembly elections, 4 Muslims contested from the Congress out of which 3 won, 4 from the Telugu Desam party (TDP) out of which 1 won and 14 from the Praja Rajyam Party out of which none won the assembly elections. However there were only two candidates from the Telangana region who contested the elections, but they failed to win any seats. He observed that after 2009, as they approached the formation of a separate state, parties became reluctant to give tickets to Muslim candidates.

He further observed that in Telangana communal polarisation is near-complete. The Khammam and Warangal districts are the least communal because of the presence of the "Andhra culture" and Left parties, while Mahabubnagar is the most communal. All other districts lie in between with varying degrees of polarisation around specific issues, which are locally relevant.[7] For instance, in Nalgonda we found that people at large, including the journalists, believe that it is the hub and "hot-bed of ISI (Inter-Services Intelligence) activities". When we cross-checked this with a Muslim Doctor Zakir Hussain, he dismissed it and argued "how can a small town like Nalgonda have such activities, they can easily be caught, but people continue to believe these rumours".

To check these kind of ISI activities, Hindus, primarily students, launched a "Modi Sena", along the lines of Shiv Sena.[8] This polarisation is not merely in elections but on the economic front as well where contracts are not given to Muslims, customers do not buy from Muslim owned shops and Anees Muqthadar, said "I have even heard that Hindu and Muslim children sit separately in schools in Nizamabad district". Earlier, Abdullah, a school teacher, pointed out that "Muslims get naturally ghettoised because they wish to live around a Masjid, where they do *namaaz* for five times a day, and a Masjid cannot be built next to a temple in a Hindu dominated colony".

Whereas, Kodandram, chairman of the TJAC, observed that Muslims in the Andhra region got integrated after they lost their distinct identity, including their language Urdu. "How is that less communal?" In fact, he believes that the movement for a separate state has opened up space for dialogue with the Muslims, perhaps for the first time. They took an active part and even took leadership positions. "There are now forums for them to air their views", reminded Kodandram.

This enthusiasm, however, seems to be limited to middle class Muslims, who do feel that in Telangana they would get social, economic and in due course even political opportunities. For instance, Md Abdul Wahab, a leading lawyer, was worried about the land value in Telangana that was very high, as the rich from Andhra bought up all the land. Similarly, he observed that, "while all the judges are from the Andhra region, all the peons are from the Telangana region in the Courts". He believed that Telangana will bring better employment opportunities for the next generation, drinking water, water for irrigation, among other things.

Md Wahab felt that people are not communal in their everyday life; it is only during elections that they get polarised. As an example, he pointed out that the majority of his clients were in fact Hindus.[9] However, the gap between the middle class and lower rungs in Muslim society is so wide that it is difficult to say whether those who are enthusiastic should be treated more as middle class respondents and less as Muslim respondents. Or can one reach the conclusion that better economic opportunities, which are what Telangana promises to bring will positively impact the Muslim society by creating a more enlarged middle class among them.

Political Parties and Telangana Muslims

It is important to note that the Telangana issue is visualised quite differently by various political parties. While the TRS and to some extent even the Congress views it as a case of "internal colonisation" by the Andhra capital, the Communist party of India (CPI) sees it as a case of "backwardness" due to uneven growth intrinsic to capitalism. and the BJP views it as a case of small state and cultural assertion against alien-Muslim-rule. All parties are now, after the formation of Telangana, speaking a language of inclusive development. However within this frame, the social section that has received the least attention and has fallen through the cracks is that of Muslims.

While Muslims perceive political representation as the most important solution for them, political parties have become increasingly hesitant as they suspect the winnability factor of a Muslim candidate, and Telangana is witnessing an immediate consolidation and polarisation of Hindu votes wherever a Muslim candidate is given a ticket. In the outgoing assembly with the total strength of 294 members, there are only 11 Muslim members. They include seven from Hyderabad (all from MIM) and one each from Anantapur, Chitoor, Kadapa, and Guntur districts. There is just one Muslim MP (from MIM) out of 42 Lok Sabha members from the state in the outgoing house. (Jafri: 2014)

Telangana Rashtra Samithi

In fact, the TRS supremo K. Chandrashekhar Rao (KCR) made a rather uncanny public announcement that no Muslim would be given a ticket from the TRS in 2014 assembly elections as "they cannot win elections". He added that he could think of giving them tickets in the next assembly elections. Similarly,

KCR had earlier announced that a Muslim would be made the deputy chief minister but later retracted his statement. After these announcements and the previous history related to the candidature of Ibrahim, Muslims are suspicious about the TRS and KCR in particular. Many Muslim respondents said that though KCR is not explicitly communal, he is certainly not a "reliable character". Muslims feel that the TRS will finally go with the BJP, and many cited the instance of Narendra (a former MP with the BJP and a known face of the RSS) joining the TRS. Though it is another matter that the BJP has finally aligned with the TDP, and the TRS and the Congress are fighting the 2014 Lok Sabha elections on their own.

Lok Janshakti Party

Shahadat Ali, who is himself an active member of the Lok Janshakti Party (LJP), argued that the BJP is not the only communal party in Telangana. and that all other parties are following "undeclared Hindutva" by denying seats and not helping Muslims win elections. He pointed out that though there is communal polarisation in other states such as Uttar Pradesh, "but how come in every elections not less than 30 MLAs who are Muslims win elections, and in Telangana not even a single Muslim candidate wins". He felt that the BJP only stokes feelings that exist among the general public and in other political parties. He pointed to how the BJP is now mobilising unemployed youth by organising Hanuman Jayanthi, and the "Modi phenomenon" is helping them consolidate the Hindu vote.

However, it looked like that the overwhelming majority of Muslims had decided to cast their votes for the Congress, which is what they have been doing in the past; as one of the respondents said voting for Congress "is now a habit for Muslims". The Congress under Rajshekar Reddy proposed 4% reservations for Muslims in jobs and educational institutions, while TRS promised 12%. Though the Andhra Pradesh High Court struck the proposition down, it is pending before the Supreme Court.

Majlis Ittehadul Muslimeen

In all of this, the MIM party stands at the other end of the spectrum. The MIM was the only party, along with the Communist Party of India (Marxist) (CPM), which explicitly and openly opposed the formation of a separate state of Telangana. The MIM argued all through that formation of Telangana will strengthen the Sangh Parivar. They have a more aggressive posturing towards the majoritarianism of other political parties. One of their supporters Hasan Kalim, a school assistant said, "Muslims have been robbed by the Hindus, so why should Muslims feel if Telangana Hindus are in turn being robbed by the Hindus from the Andhra region".

MIM has so far exclusively focused on contesting only from the old city area of Hyderabad. In the previous elections it had won 7 seats in the assembly and the leader of MIM Assaduddin Owaisi won 1 MP seat. In the districts, MIM generally supports other political parties such as the TDP or the Congress depending on the situation. Muslims themselves in the district do not vote for the MIM either, because they cannot win seats on their own or because of an overwhelming fear that voting for the MIM invites anger and also possible attack from the Hindu community. One of the respondents said, "If we vote for the MIM in the municipal elections, there is always the fear of a Hindu backlash".

In fact, in the public meeting of the MIM that we attended in course of the survey, Assaduddin Owaisi made an explicit reference to this in arguing that "if you do not vote for the MIM out of fear of the Hindus, then remember tomorrow when the BJP and the Sangh Parivar grows there will be no one to blame except yourselves". He made a plea to Muslims to overcome their fear. Abdul Shafiq, a junior lawyer, pointed out that by supporting MIM, "we might win a few seats of ward members in the corporation but who will protect us after that".

While the Hindus pointed out, that it is the MIM which encourages sectarian mobilisation. They often cited the speech by the younger brother of Asaduddin, Akbaruddin Owaisi, who made an inciting speech where he claimed that "if police remain mute spectators, Muslims in India can finish off the Hindus in less than 15 minutes". Following which, Akbaruddin Owaisi was arrested. Similarly, others pointed out that the MIM does not allow any other political party to campaign in the old city and has a complete grip over the Muslims in this area.

The editor of *Siyasat*, a popular news daily in Urdu, pointed out that the real reason why the MIM opposed the formation of Telangana was because they have business deals with Andhra politicians, especially land deals. Much of the Waqf Board lands are occupied by Andhra builders and they pay a cut in exchange of that to the MIM. The MIM itself indulges in land grabbing and extends loans to poor Muslims and extracts a high rate of interest.

However, Jafri, the ideologue of MIM, pointed out that the reason for MIMs opposition to the formation of the new state was that if backwardness was the reason for the formation of Telangana, then Rayalseema too is backward, and therefore MIM demanded "Rayala Telangana" that also includes a sizeable population of the Muslims. Similarly, he also pointed out that as part of de-limitation many of the Muslim-dominated areas are being reserved for scheduled castes. The long-term agenda of the MIM is to forge an alliance between the party and dalits and the OBCs so that the hold of dominant Reddy and Velema castes is reduced. Further, he pointed out that the MIM is powerful in Hyderabad and the bifurcation creates a problem for the status of Hyderabad city.

Conclusions

To conclude, the plight of Muslims is rather worrying in Telangana. They are socially ostracised, politically marginalised and economically weak. In spite of this, the majority community continues to perceive them as a threat and as aggressive. In fact, they believe, as one of the Hindu respondent said, "Muslims are quiet because they have been 'put in their place', otherwise they will begin to dominate the Hindus".[10] Due to this perceived idea, there is no general sympathy for the Muslims.

Various Muslim organisations have therefore demanded "reserved seats" as per their population, on a similar pattern as seats are reserved for the dalits. This they feel is the only way that Muslim leadership can emerge and change the existing plight, the way dalit leadership has done. Throughout the survey, many respondents drew parallels between the situation of Muslims and Dalits, and even urged for a similar act as the

Scheduled Castes and the Scheduled Tribes (Prevention of Atrocities) Act, in order to prevent the everyday attacks and humiliation of Muslims. Anees Muqthadar said, "as dalits cannot win from a general constituency even today, Muslim cannot win elections from a general constituency".

However, in contrast to this parallel, Riaz, the general secretary of Mahajan Socialist Front pointed out that "there is a possibility of dalits gradually shifting to BJP. In Mahabubnagar they have already formed BJP Dalit Morcha". Alongside, physical safety and security remains their primary concern. It is intriguing that none of the respondents referred to either corruption or inflation as a major concern in the forthcoming elections. How democratic Telangana is going to be squarely depends on how inclusive it is going to be towards its Muslim population.

REFERENCES

Gudavarthy, Ajay (2014): "Small States, Big Problems", *The Hindu*, 13 March, available at http://www.thehindu.com/opinion/lead/small-states-big-problems/article5774395.ece, accessed on 25 April 2014.

Jafri, Amin (2014): "Hard Choices for Minorities in 2014 Elections" *Times of India*, 10 February, available at http://timesofindia.indiatimes.com/city/hyderabad/Hard-choices-for-minorities-in-2014-elections/articleshow/30126219.cms, accessed on 25 April 2014.

PTI (2011): "Celebrate September 17 as Telangana Liberation Day, Demands BJP", *The Hindu*, 6 September, available at http://www.thehindu.com/news/national/andhra-pradesh/celebrate-sept-17-a..., accessed on 25 April 2014.

Rao, C.H. Hanumantha (2014): "The New Telangana State: A Perspective for Inclusive and Sustainable Development", *Economic and Political Weekly*, 1 March, 49(9): 10-13, available at http://www.epw.in/commentary/new-telangana-state.html, accessed on 25 April 2014.

NOTES

1. The survey was carried out from 21st March to 25th March, 2014.
2. Communal polarisation, some pointed out, sharpened in 1977 when a history-sheeter, Erra Satyam, organised communal riots

in Mahbubnagar. It is an irony that the town of Mahbubnagar and its central market place greets with a statue of Erra Satyam located prominently.

3. To counter this and organise a show of strength, Muslims organised "Muslim gharjana" in 2012 in Mabubnagar, where it was claimed about 10,000 Muslims took part. This was in support of Telangana, and against the wrong kind of propaganda against the Muslim community.
4. Dr. Zakir Husain claimed that Osmania General Hospital in its hey days before 1948 was ranked 6th globally.
5. One Muslim respondent thought that if communal riots take place, Maoists will gain ground in Telangana.
6. Riaz, General Secretary of Mahajan Socialist Party, who is also contesting elections in Warangal, pointed out that 12 Muslim students committed suicide, though it is against Koran.
7. Waheeb, a journalist with *Etemaad,* a news daily close to the MIM, felt that Warangal was less communal because of a large number of Dargahs, "where Hindus and Muslims even today go together".
8. More recently, a film actor Pawan Kalyan, who had declared support for Narendra Modi, launched his new political outfit by the name, "Jan Sena".
9. In a lighter vein he added that Hindus think a Muslim lawyer will be more sincere in fighting their case, and vice versa. Similarly, Zakir Husain, a doctor in Nalgonda district, pointed out that a large number of his clients were Hindus.
10. Bhaktha Vatsal, another Hindu respondent felt that "in the old city area, Muslims drive and come in the wrong way, and if you object to that, they begin to abuse you". This is one of the very popular perceptions about how Muslims in the old city, near Charminar behave with the Hindus.

Published in the *Economic and Political Weekly*
(Web Exclusives) Vol. XLIX, No. 17, April 26, 2014.

AAP AND GRAFT

16

Anna Hazare's Soap Opera

Anna Hazare's anti-graft movement is now part of the growing epic predicament that Indian democracy seems to be increasingly drifting towards. An epic predicament, like any major epic of India such as the Ramayan or Mahabharath, is a moment where we know the end result but or precisely because of that our interest in the phenomenon sustains. We all knew watching Ramayan who would win and why, yet the story keeps us spellbound and of course glued to the television when it was telecast. Not the suspense but its predictability is what endears it, and makes it so familiar. In a democracy marked by everyday uncertainty, here is movement that promises radical change without any risk, pain or unpredictable overtures, which is what only an epic can do. It promises drastic change without shocking us, and in fact adhering and confirming to the dominant values in the society. We all for sure know that the Lokpal bill, even if passed, cannot in any significant measure contain corruption in our country, since corruption is a lot more structural and has its roots in the nature of the political economy, yet we are in no position to brush it aside as a wave but hope against hope expecting it to deliver what it is actually promising to do.

The proportion and the scope of corruption have grown manifold post economic reforms and opening up of the economy. It is both due to the manner in which reforms have been introduced and initiated in India best described by Jenkin's as 'reforms by stealth', and also the changes it brought to our economy from being an agrarian economy to the sudden rise of the rent-seeking class that dominates the state.

Today the economy and its high growth owes a lot to these newly emergent middle men like classes that are neither an industrial class nor make profits out of manufacturing basic or any other good.

Instead they make big money out of contracts of various kinds. The state is therefore dominated by the rising 'contractor class' including civil, liquor, real estate and more recently the mining contractors best typified by the infamous Reddy Brothers of Karnataka. In fact, a bulk of state revenues is today generated from and by this contractor class. The State needs them as much as they need the state.

What we identify as corruption is the only way these classes and state can mutually mediate and survive. The old distinction between the economic and political class is collapsing, with these classes themselves entering and controlling the state, as part of its executive organ. In fact, it wouldn't perhaps be an exaggeration if one were to mark the shift of the Indian state from being *a contractual state to a contractor state.* The nature of the capital is speculative, and that makes this class indifferent to longterm planning and democratic procedures, it instead relies more on quick and speculative modes for making profits. It is these changes in the nature of the political economy that are inextricably linked to the growing phenomenon of both corporate corruption and that by public officials. There is very little that Anna's Lokpal Bill can do about setting right this structural limitation, yet it sustains our interest and looks indispensable for a democracy to deliver whatever it can afford to. More importantly those sections of the society including the democratic, progressive, and in some cases radical organisations, are in no position to oppose the movement, knowing very well what it promises is way too exaggerated.

This is what frames the response of these sections, as a tempered and essentially a simulated exercise.

Simulation or epic predicament, I believe, is part of the very nature of popular democracy, and those who understand this make good use of it, as Advani did with his initial Rath Yatra to Ayodhya meticulously organised with the tele serial Ramayan as the backdrop, and his recent Jan Chetna Yatra with Anna's soap opera in the background. Popular democracy appeals at the level of intention and not merely evidence, and this is so with any epic that cannot be questioned with any amount of archaeological or textual evidence, as witnessed with not just the Ayodhya temple but the more recent controversy around 'Many Ramayanas' in Delhi University. There was nothing particularly communal about the teleserial Ramayan but the context resignified it into a footage for Hindutva, as Anna's movement is a worthy cause in itself but the current context entails more than what meets the eye, and way too complex to either reject or whole heartedly accept it. Each entails its own consequence, and also partly explains the massive confusion amongst individuals and political organisations of various ideological hues in terms of its implications for democracy, and for the ruling elite of the nation.

The Left of Centre and progressive and radical forces are caught in the dilemma that they have been part of since the days of the death of the 'developmental state'. In the hey days of the developmental state the Left in India had a safe and a promising posture of critiquing the state itself, and took upon themselves the responsibility of indiscriminately delegitimizing it, but once the period of neoliberal reforms began, they were caught unawares as their job has been taken up more robustly and vigorously by the corporates and their associates including the media. They are aware that any excessive critique of the state and public officials only further legitimises and entrenches the global corporate model of development. They are caught with the unenviable position of critiquing the state without delegitimising it to the extent that we lay a red carpet welcome to the global corporate. They cannot whole heartedly side with Anna since it does not raise the issue of corruption by the corporate, nor can they oppose it since they share his angst and concern for the decaying democracy and the moribund state that is best reflected in the mammoth corruption it's ruling elite is structurally dependent on and willy nilly encourages for its own survival. Corporate encourages growth and efficiency, while state is all about corruption is an argument not agreeable to them, and they had the same dilemma while supporting the RTI. The choice they seem to have is to extend measured support while cautioning against exaggerated expectations, which is not an attractive position to take when the mood of the nation is swept with emotional appeal of the movement marked by a sense of hope in times that look increasingly desperate and stagnant. The only other choice is to offer a critique, the way Arundhati Roy did, that only looks absolutist and unrealistic, if not irrelevant. The problem with absolutist critique, however relevant analysis it might offer, is it gives no terms to negotiate but only out rightly rejects the struggle, since it believes it does not say much about poverty, Greenhunt, and state repression. These are of course terms that are outside the scope of this struggle, and how does one evaluate a critique that does not engage with a movement for what it is, and a critique that can be extended to anything and everything?

The liberal democrats, on the other hand, are worried that Anna's movement undermines democratic procedures and representative institutions, including and above all the Parliament. Nobody, according to them, is above public representatives, and undercutting procedures and deliberation in a democracy can be dangerous. Thus, civil society can play a complementary role and cannot supplant democratic institutions, which amounts to undermining democracy itself. They were therefore unhappy with the so called'blackmail' tactics by team Anna and raised the pertinent question as to who are team Anna accountable to? And what if those appointed to the Lokpal are themselves corrupt? But here again the story is not so simple. We are today witnessing a strange irony where procedures and the end less delay they entail are used by the ruling elite as a shield against being prosecuted. They escape hiding in the interstices of the time lag that procedure of checks and balances offer in a representative democracy.

However, this does not mean democracy can work without elaborate procedures and checks, since even with all of this we routinely are witness to the brazen abuse of organisations that need to maintain their autonomy and anonymity, including the way CBI is used (which prompted some in the BJP to refer to it as Congress Bureau of India!). It is a case of democracy turning against itself. Here again they seem to have no easy choice, the liberal voices struggled to distance themselves from those in the ruling party, especially the likes of Digvijay Singh.

Perhaps, it's the right wing that managed to put up the best show, not in the least because they are any serious about rooting out corruption in the system. The Right headed by the BJP to begin with had an easy run since they are in the opposition, and it helps them to corner, by whatever means, the dispensation of the day. It also could afford a more wholehearted support to the movement since they could sense that the spectacle of Anna had all the elements that are usually part of the repertoire of the right wing's modes of mobilisation in India. The performative aspect of Anna's spectacle included his ascetic living, bachelorhood, use of slogans like 'Vande Mataram', and 'Bharat Mata ki jai', which whether intended or not, come a tad too close to the persona of any RSS pracharak, in spite of his Gandhian believes. This again is what is strange of Indian democracy. The symbolic can easily subvert the content, because content without the symbolic can be reduced to the synthetic. It is this gloss alongside the commonsensical propositions and the naivety of Anna that is often confused for simplicity in Indian public discourse, well suited the mobilisational modes of the Right. Anna's soap opera was a Bollywood style hero versus anti-hero narrative that goes well with Hindu versus Muslim, or Ram versus Ravan type popular narrative style that has distinct and identifiable symbols of good and bad. This indeed is a rich resource, again in the neo liberal times where the targets have become transnational and therefore invisible. To bring alive something that is silent, invisible or dead can be very empowering in the populist mode that democracy works within.

Now, finally we can raise the more difficult question as to why did Congress as the ruling dispensation respond with such alacrity. The arguments offered as to because of the mass mobilisation and the pressure it could build, or the moral pressure that fasting can bring are, to my mind, insufficient to explain the way they buckled under pressure. If these were the reasons then how could Congress so blatantly ignore the struggle for a separate state of Telangana that witnessed unprecedented mobilisation in every nook and cranny of its districts; if a hunger strike is effective because its the land of Gandhi holds any truth, then how do we explain the sheer negligence of the suffering by Irom Sharmila for well over a decade now? Congress is not even open to a debate and the blockade in Manipur amounted to nothing more than another day's news, not to mention the way Omar Abdullah has been bargaining for piecemeal withdrawal of AFSPA. The answer could well lie in the social base that got attracted to the anti graft movement. While there is some truth in the fact that people from all walks of life, and all classes, including people from rural hinterlands in the North supported the movement, it was primarily a movement that gained support from the professionals and urban rich with keen interest avowed by the NRIs. Their interest overlapped with the belief not only that a corruption free India would directly benefit them but also that India would become a more attractive destination for global investments. Better infrastructure, work culture, and violence free India with a strong 'law and order', at any cost, it is believed, would enrich the global image of India and would move a step closer to being a super power that it can in a foreseeable future. In this frame a corruption free India is a cause worth fighting, notwithstanding how much of the growth and prosperity of these classes is due to prevalent corrupt practices in the system. This anomaly could not hold these classes back and instead it is their firm belief of serving national (read global) interests that motivated these privileged sections of urban India that propelled them to occupy the streets that have been, for some time now, vacated by the poor who with growing distress levels, it seems, have little time for protest politics at their disposal. Again, ironically this dream of India going global was initiated by Congress itself, and by more than anyone else by Prime Minister Manmohan Singh himself. But then this precisely is the reason for the protest.

Democracy has again this strange dimension where, within a fractured polity, parties and governments are identified with a constructed social base, and are expected to be loyal to that base. Today, while there is enough pressure that governments are supposed to represent all sections of the society but we seem to be reconciled to fact that they rule in the name of certain sections and which in turn, it is expected, will benefit everyone. It seems, in contemporary Indian democracy, it is not so much of an issue if governments fail to keep the promise of representing everyone's interests, as conflict of interest looks like an irreducible fact of modern democracies, but it does assume eruptive proportions when governments fail to serve the agenda of the class and sections of the society they actually work on behalf of in reality. Congress under Manmohan Singh, notwithstanding its elaborate welfare regime, always projected itself as a government in favour of the private, and global corporate capital, and professionals working for it. When corruption,as they perceive, hurts their interests, and Congress looks reluctant to act then it is construed as not only an inefficient government in power but also a party that is betraying and disloyal to its own stated ideals and social base. It is now a more important criterion for efficiency and democracy to stand to one's stated ideals and represent its distinct social base, however partisan it might be, than to be actually democratic in terms of representing all conflicting interests. We might be actually, as a society, getting reconciled to this partisan nature of democracy rather than expecting it to be close to its ideal type functioning. It therefore makes for dramatic change in the democratic current whenever parties or individuals representing them overstep the brief they have offered the polity. There is therefore more uproar when Advani makes what were considered pro-Jinnah comments, without much interest shown in the veracity of the historical truth or accuracy of these observations. Even if what Advani observed about Jinnah were to be historically true, coming from him makes them false. He could never perhaps recover the stature he enjoyed before those comments, however well meaning they might be or however desperate he might be to switch to a more moderate image in the interest of the future prospects of his party. Similarly, the CPM could never recover from the damage it inflicted upon itself after they ostensibly betrayed the very peasants it had once mobilised.

This betrayal, even if it involves a move in the positive direction, is seen in popular democracy as graft.

Chandrababu Naidu in Andhra Pradesh, after he began to raise the issues of the farmers, came to be looked upon as a more cunning and opportunistic politician, than when he proudly projected himself as a CEO of the state and pronounced the irrelevance of agriculture and history. What Congress therefore faced was a crisis from 'within' its own social base, and it is this anxiety of loss of a image it constructed and stood by that propelled it to take Anna's movement so seriously and begin to work towards a possible resolution. The same Prime Minister, who has worked overtime not to respond to a popular movement like Telangana, went to the extent of dissolving his government over the nuclear deal. This is not the pressure of democratic mobilisation, even if it is a part of the logic, but more an implosion from within that politics seems to be succumbing to. Anna's movement appealed to the 'dominant' social, as against mass, base of the ruling party and it could ill afford to ignore, lest it looks inefficient and 'corrupt'.

It is this drama marked by compounded confusion that gave Anna's movement a larger than life image, and an aura of a epic, where merely knowing and harping on the outcome is not only insufficient but actually contributes in making it the epic soap opera it has become. The saga might be now running its last few episodes, but will nevertheless continue to engage us till it comes to be replaced by a more enthralling soap opera where not merely the subject but even the actors might have to be new and fresh but predictable.

Published as Working Paper Series #9, Institute for Global Law and Policy, Harvard Law School, December 2011.

17

In Defence of the Politician

Harbans Mukhia's article in *The Hindu*, "Making it 'for the people' again" (Op-Ed, October 13, 2012), has endorsed the campaign against graft led by Arvind Kejriwal as a movement that has the potential to make democracy once again "for the people."

He argues that the movement highlights the growing crisis of legitimacy "of the whole system of governance" and squarely re-strengthens democracy and the democratic content of public institutions by making them more accountable, in tilting them in favour of the "99 per cent." While the article correctly notes that what is legal, like the Emergency of 1975, need not necessarily be legitimate, it assumes, however, that what is popular is unambiguously democratic and singular.

The problem with campaigns such as Anna Hazare's and now Mr. Kejriwal's is that they assume a seamless continuity between social campaigns and political mobilisation. If one is serious about democracy, one cannot afford to overlook the consequences of these two different plains and their implications for democracy. While it is easy to correlate popular will with social activism against corruption, the moment it enters political/electoral politics the dynamics undergo dramatic transformation. It is relatively easy to generate consent and consensus in the social domain especially against issues such as corruption; every individual and social group can afford to concede the point that corruption is illegitimate, morally degrading and undermines democracy. However, politics has to do with concrete interests and wider social, and cultural beliefs and prejudices of individuals and social groups and does not have the privilege to pick and choose issues. This is where democracy is a far more complex game than what we are given to believe by Mr. Kejriwal, and academics like Prof. Mukhia and Yogendra Yadav.

If democracy is all about articulating and representing popular will, then one needs to be equally concerned about the content of that popular will. When the popular is not democratic in content but popular amounts to democracy, how does one work towards reconciliation between the two? The recent spate of events in Haryana, and the pronouncements by the leaders of the Khap panchayats, which found resonance in the views expressed by the Ministers in the Congress government, explains the inherent conflict within democratic processes. In this case what is popular and "by the people" is not necessarily democratic in content, but political leaders are expected to represent the popular will, and to that extent were "legitimate" in expressing the popular beliefs of the constituency they represent. Politics, therefore, unlike social campaigns, cannot have the privilege of selectively picking and choosing issues that are perceived to be unproblematically and morally correct, and can generate consensus.

Nature of Democracy

Politics includes everything from the public to the private, and the nature of democracy is decided by how politicians respond and negotiate between multiple issues that are often conflicting. It is for this reason that we expect politicians to have an opinion on everything. It is pertinent while talking of democracy to remember that not only is the popular not necessarily democratic but "the people" are not necessarily united but have conflicting interests. Politics and democracy are essentially an art of generating a consensus-majority amidst these conflicting interests, on the one hand, and negotiating and representing social views that are uneven—sometimes democratic but frequently regressive on the other.

Corruption, therefore, has roots not merely in the economy but also in the nature of the polity and society itself. It is in negotiating with what could sometimes be irreconcilable differences between social groups, and in accommodating interests that cannot be easily accommodated, that corruption finds its place in what we often refer to as populist and corrupt measures, including offering money, liquor, and other imaginative and sometimes unimaginable sops.

Again, while Prof. Mukhia is right in pointing out that we have adopted an economic model that impoverished the majority, even here it has impoverished different social groups to different extents and in different ways. The ways the tribals of Chhattisgarh have got displaced and impoverished is markedly different from the way the backward classes have been treated. People always perceive inequality not in absolute terms but in relative terms, and it is for this reason that even the urban middle classes feel they have had it rough with economic reforms. Democracy heightens and brings into play these nuances and uneven impacts that are not imagined but real. How to tilt the popular will in favour of the poorest and the most deprived keeping these open, conflicting and representative mechanisms in place is the real challenge and the most effective way of "making it for the people again"—and not in generating a moralistic critique of politics and politicians holding a moral high ground for generating consensus through social activism and around selectively and prudently chosen issues.

Undermining this difference, far from strengthening democracy will actually undermine it. Imagining a simplistic consensus "for the people" has always given rise to authoritarian regimes, which is what partially explains why all campaigns against graft, even in the past, have tilted towards right-wing modes of mobilisation, including that led by Jayaprakash Narayan. Politicians of the day need to be critiqued and held accountable but the avocation of politics and the creative image and role of a politician in a democracy need to be avowedly defended.

Published in *The Hindu*, October 15, 2012.

18

AAP: Surviving Politics

The stunning debut by the Aam Aadmi Party (AAP) in the recent Delhi elections has taken everyone by surprise. None of the exit polls predicted this, nor that the electorate would look at AAP as an alternative. AAP is a new experiment in the way it opened up space for honest candidates even if inexperienced in electoral politics. It inaugurated a bottom-up organisational structure, based on the principle of voluntary participation, and has maintained transparency in collecting funds. While these are laudable practices unheard of in the history of Indian electoral politics, are they sufficient markers for a political party to survive and play a long innings?

AAP's rise can be attributed to the general discontent among the electorate, of being taken for granted, of voting along predisposed lines, of inherited political affiliations. However, the discontent is also due to the growing inequality, the lack of employment, everyday harassment by police and state officials and, of course, inflation. And corruption has emerged as symbolic of all these issues. Thus, in a discourse against corruption everyone can see what they wish to. It is precisely this reason that gave AAP its win in higher middle class localities, such as South and New Delhi, and in the reserved constituencies as well. AAP could project these varied fragments of discontent into a cohesive political articulation of the people (*aam admi*) versus the state. It is along the lines in which civil society was constructed in Eastern Europe after the collapse of the old regime, where 'people' are civil society and 'corrupt officials/politicians' are the state. This discourse construes 'the people' as a single datum. The corrective mechanisms to address this discontent are seen as a new set of institutional mechanisms, including the Lok Pal Bill, the right to recall, NOTA, compulsory voting, limits on and transparency in corporate funding of political parties, among other issues. Here again, corruption becomes symbolic of the discontent, the changes becoming symbolic of a new system.

That's the easy part. However, the real stuff of politics happens when parties begin to address schisms that exist in society, when they are called on to accommodate conflicting interests. Here, a mere discourse on corruption or a language of institutional change cannot hold conflicting demands together because these discourses are neither the source nor the solution to the nature of the problems faced by various social groups. How can this discourse pacify conflicting interests between the 'people' of Telangana and those of Seemandhra? Or between those who demand reservations and expansion of affirmative action policies and those who resist this as being counter-productive in building a globally competitive nation? Between those who are dispossessed by the new economic model and those who stand to gain with an exponential rise in incomes?

As of now, AAP has no considered position on any of these issues. In fact, we might recollect that, during the campaign lead by Anna Hazare, Prashant Bhusan had taken a position in favour of the Right to Self-determination for the people of Kashmir and had spoken in favour of Gilani and Arundhati Roy, while Anna and the rest of his team were quick to distance themselves from such a position. It is in addressing issues of this kind that maintaining an easy consensus of the kind that can be generated around a moral issue such as corruption is extremely difficult. Once such differences come to the fore, the idealism against corruption will give way to locating differences among the *'aam admi'* and their specific locations around class, caste, gender and religion—people will again articulate their interests through such identities and not merely celebrate them. Politics is about diligently representing and accommodating conflicting interests and yet managing to generate a majority. Representation and numbers are euphemistic symbols of this underlying process. Radical change has to deeply engage with this existing reality. Idealism has to stare at and not look away from this irksome image of democracy finding its feet in India.

In celebrating the resounding victory of AAP, we need to be cautious about this context, which gets reflected in the complex patterns that have emerged across the four states. We must note that people have voted in big numbers and have voted back to power two incumbent governments in Chhattisgarh and Madhya Pradesh, in recognition of the welfare policies in both the states. Here it is continuity over dramatic change; it is measured voting over rampant discontent. At the same time, the electorate has rejected the government in Rajasthan, which was also inaugurating similar welfare schemes but might have failed in effective communication, always construed as arrogance. While in Delhi there was 'good governance', it did not translate into good politics. It could well have been a suspicion that giving a fourth term would make the government indifferent to the people, while it is always easy to draw concessions and welfare from a party that has stayed out of power for long. The reasons continue to be local and context specific and this is where the strength of Indian democracy remains. It is within this mosaic that one needs to locate and celebrate the success story of AAP.

Published in *The Hindu*, December 15, 2013.

19

Modi and Kejriwal: The Seamlessness of Difference

In the run-up to the recent election in Delhi, many surveys observed an interesting resolve of the electorates to vote for Mr. Kejriwal in Delhi and Mr. Narendra Modi in the ensuing general election. A couple of months ago, in an interactive session with the media, the Aam Aadmi Party (AAP) leader Yogendra Yadav had admitted that the majority of Delhi-ites, who wanted Mr. Kejriwal as the Chief Minister, would vote for Mr. Modi in the general election. He had also said that ever since Mr. Modi had been appointed the Bharatiya Janata Party's prime ministerial candidate, the youth vote has moved in favour of the Gujarat Chief Minister.

While it is evident that what each of these leaders represents is not only different but also a very conflicting idea of politics, the electorate feels no compunction in choosing the two together. While Mr. Kejriwal stands for a more open, approachable and participatory ethos, Mr. Modi symbolises authoritarianism, aggressive masculinity, and the sheer concentration of power. What then explains the seamless continuity that the electorate could mark between them? It is important to make sense of this in order to understand the emerging dynamics in Indian democracy.

First, this mode of choice makes it possible to argue that the vote and hyperbole around the success of the AAP is more of a negative vote against the incumbent governments and their methods of functioning rather than a positive vote for the AAP. The electorate seems to be less enamoured by the "alternative" that the AAP stands for (in any case there is no clarity as to what their concrete programme is, apart from fighting against corruption), and are voting and supporting more to insult, humiliate and insinuate the existing power blocs, political parties and their leadership. The electorate is increasingly refusing to be used as cannon fodder for the established political parties, marking a steady decline in their capacity, through their conventional organisational tactics and methods, to mobilise the electorate. It is rejecting the idea of established leadership, and the continuity this brings. The defeat of Sheila Dikshit and many other established and well known leaders, who had won many elections on the trot in Delhi, is a case in point to validate this. In this sense, the strategy of the AAP to field candidates against the top leadership of other political parties, including the much hyped contest between Rahul Gandhi and Kumar Vishwas in Amethi, is geared towards appealing to this growing sentiment among the electorate. It is therefore understandable that those who have voted for the AAP also find in Mr. Modi a similar symbol of change and an untested case that requires to be given an opportunity, more than a positive vote for what Mr. Modi's brand of politics stands for. Mr. Modi also ostensibly stands for unconventional methods in decision-making, against dynasty politics, and as somebody who is not bogged down by the niceties of institutional procedures. By that logic, he too, like the AAP, becomes an anti-establishment symbol. Both the voting patterns seem to emerge from a negative vote against the establishment that the Congress has come to represent in this case.

Realism

Thus, Mr. Modi and Mr. Kejriwal share the same discontent. Therefore, it is of little interest in whether or not the AAP is fielding a candidate against Mr. Modi. Even if they eventually decide to do so (since there is still speculation as to where Mr. Modi would contest from), for all we know, he might come out with flying colours as he might stand to represent, in popular perception, the more aggressive, ardent and effective voice against the establishment.

Second, there is a deep sense of pragmatism, or realism, in both Mr. Modi and Mr. Kejriwal's brand of politics. For Mr.

Kejriwal, "Swaraj" stands, for effective service-delivery mechanisms, beyond the pulls of ideology. He has repeatedly said he is neither right nor left but an *aam aadmi,* and would do anything that fixes the everyday problems of the *aam aadmi.*

The AAP, in his own words, is *"shivji ka baarath,"* where everyone and with all kinds of persuasions are welcome. Mr. Modi epitomises this similar kind of pragmatic approach to politics. He is here to deliver, and make administration effective, even if he is aggressive, autocratic and concentrates power, since these might be necessary to make the "system" efficient. Any debate on ideology and the values involved in pushing the system look like a drag, and less important than the pressing need for things to get done. Neither of them has campaigned on the basis of a concrete programme, economic or social. While Mr. Kejriwal has promised to get things done in days—15 days for the Lokpal—Mr. Modi has claimed there are now only 100 days to turn India around, and fast pace it.

Representing the Popular

Third, there is an unsuspecting idea of the popular in both leaders. They both appeal to unleashing the popular in its raw and undiluted form. They believe in articulating, more directly, the popular sentiment of the people. While Mr. Modi champions the majoritarian instinct in the popular, Mr. Kejriwal takes recourse to the symbolism of the *"aam aadmi"* that is also constructed as a majority. It is popular because it is the majority. While Mr. Kejriwal takes recourse to the rhetoric of direct democracy, Mr. Modi has already proved himself in Gujarat, in letting the majority community directly settle scores. Added to that is his credibility in being voted back thrice to power. The logic often used by his supporters is: "If he has done anything wrong then why would the majority of the electorate vote him back? The *aam aadmi* too has his share of prejudices, be it caste, religion, gender or race; neither of them would pause to ask if everything in the popular is necessarily democratic. While Mr. Modi found a friend in the popular voice of Lata Mangeshkar, the AAP has been happy to settle for Kumar Vishwas and his populist brand of comedy. While Mr. Modi has actively stoked prejudices, the AAP, at best, has left them unaddressed and unresolved. The party's recent position on *khap* panchayats is a clear indication of this cultivated ambiguity. While there is no possibility of taking recourse to celebrating the cult of the subaltern unproblematically, both Mr. Modi and Mr. Kejriwal thrive on the majoritarian instinct that drives such politics.

The media has only preoccupied itself in raising the debate between the leadership qualities of Rahul Gandhi and Mr. Modi, but if it were to only begin probing the contrast between Mr. Modi and Mr. Kejriwal, it would be intriguing to see how the viewers and eventually the electorate would begin to respond to this conundrum.

Published in *The Hindu*, February 13, 2014.

The Modi Phenomenon

20

Workings of a Modi-fied India

Indian democracy was always proclaimed to be different; to add to this difference is now the story of the run-up to the upcoming general elections that is being fought like a Presidential election around two likely candidates for the post of the Prime Minister, within a parliamentary system of democracy.

Since the time of the economic reforms, the difference in the political programme between political parties has become almost negligible, and therefore the significance of political parties has been supplanted by personalities.

One might offer a sustained critique of dynasty politics being inimical to the sensibilities of a good democracy, but the facelessness brought to the political process with all major national parties speaking a similar language of growth and development, dynasties and families at least serve the purpose for the common man of pinning down responsibilities, and demanding concessions.

It is the same context which has made individual personalities more important than even the political parties they represent. It is interesting to observe that in the conditions laid down by Nitish Kumar as to who is an acceptable candidate to lead the NDA, among other criteria he also pointed towards a person without 'rough edges'. Never before was this the case in the history of Indianelectoralpolitics.

The growing clout of the corporate sector and presence of urban middle classes has made Narendra Modi the leading choice. Added to this is the amenability of his aggressive posturing to the requirements of the media. 'Mediatisation of politics' has also made electoral politics more personality-centric than party-centric.

Though this is not a settled question as of now, since the Sangh Parivar needs to keep its options open in an era of coalition politics, and need to confirm, even if Modi is ostensibly the most popular leader, if he can sustain the confidence of other political parties, given the kind of Hindutva-brand of politics he stands for. L.K. Advani could well be the dark horse; he is already looking and sounding like a moderate.

Not very long ago he represented the Hindutva-brand of politics that Modi is now a symbol for, and his rabid posturing then lead to a consensus around Atal Bihari Vajpayee as the moderate who can sustain a coalition. There is no reason why this story cannot repeat itself, and looks like a possible way out for the likes of Nitish Kumar to keep his ties with the BJP, along with his secular credentials.

Rahul Gandhi, on the other hand, is torn between a dual power-centre model of governance, where Manmohan-Montek symbolise growth and he has, rather unsuccessfully, attempted to stand for a pro-poor rhetoric. He supported the tribals in Niamgiri, he has recently in his speech for the CII spoken of village pradhans and a bottom-up mobilisation.

Such rhetoric has to be backed by a firm model of welfare state, but what we have now in India is a string of welfare policies without a welfare regime. Welfare has been pursued only to further legitimise economic reforms, as a secondary discourse and thus Rahul Gandhi also looks like playing second fiddle and is perceived to be uninitiated.

Added to this is his disinterest in building a persona that is amenable to mediatisation. In the process, he neither symbolises a rabid reforms process and high-growth mania, like Chidambaram does, nor does he symbolise an old Mai-baap state that patronises the poor. As electoral results in Uttar Pradesh and Bihar have signified, he remains a non-symbol. What can at the most be a face-saving device for him could be his dynasty.

It is this space that then opens up for the 'Third-Front' experiment. In the consensus on economic reforms and FDI, regional parties have taken to symbolic protests, even if many of them in terms of their party programme remain committed to FDI.

While centre and the national represent the global, the regional and the states have come to represent the local, and those social groups outside the urban middle class that have not gained so much, and might stand to lose with the globalisation of the economy.

It is in context that even Chandrababu Naidu, who once epitomised the imagery of a CEO (which interestingly Modi has claimed for himself now), has of late realised the importance of agriculture and has been campaigning for the farmers in Andhra Pradesh.

It is this agenda of agriculture and the interests of local and regional capital at one level, and numbers in a coalition era that will open or close the leadership options for the likes of Mulayam Singh Yadav and Nitish Kumar.

Here, it is certainly not the personality that will be the mainstay of their campaigns. These aspirants are also less likely to find a favourable media, given their alternative agenda, and also the modality of their politics and personalities that look less swanky, and less aesthetic to a sanitised and an insular urban discourse of the media.

Published in *The Deccan Herald*, April 21, 2013.

21

Modi's Campaign of Contradictions

There has been much talk about the alleged sum of Rs. 10,000 crore being spent on Narendra Modi's campaign in creating "brand Modi," but much less attention has been paid to its content and structure. In other words, what has been the sum and substance of Mr. Modi's carefully crafted multilayered campaign?

The essence of the Bharatiya Janata Party's prime ministerial candidate's campaign seems to be based on an uncanny ability to combine overtly contradictory claims. To that extent that it has succeeded in creating a "brand Modi" that is elusive. What it has allowed is the coexistence of a mosaic of meanings, which each person, depending on his/her persuasion, can make sense of.

Contradictions

Mr. Modi claims that he does not believe in dividing society into Hindus, Muslims, Sikhs and Christians, but instead looks at them as being "125 crore Indians." He says he believed all through his stint in Gujarat that the citizens of the state were "my 6 crore Gujaratis." This rhetoric of a pan-Indian inclusiveness is combined with emphasis on development and good governance, which many of Mr. Modi's advertisements on television emphasise. Even as Mr. Modi claims all this, Amit Shah makes the infamous "badly" comment in Muzzafarnagar, which was claimed to be a "badly" not against any particular community but against the misgovernance of the Congress. Mr. Modi claims that he believes in carrying forward Atal Bihari Vajpayee's policy of "humanity, democracy and Kashmiriyat" regarding his approach to the Kashmir issue, even as the former President of the BJP, Nitin Gadkari, simultaneously makes an announcement that the party will scrap Article 370 if it manages a majority on its own.

Further, Syed Ali Shah Geelani makes a claim that Mr. Modi, in order to enhance his image, requested him to initiate a dialogue with him on Kashmir. The attempt clearly seems to be to "outsource" Hindutva to the second rung of the leadership while Mr. Modi himself maintains a stoic silence on it. Mr. Modi's own contribution to the unstated agenda has been a series of symbolic gestures (and not overt statements) that allow the creation of a chimera of meanings. These gestures include his decision to contest from Varanasi and not offer a single ticket to a Muslim candidate in Uttar Pradesh, marking a shift to a "low-intensity" communalisation.

The bulk of his campaign has been against the Gandhi family and their method of managing the party. He has criticised "dynasty politics," ridiculed the "remote control" mode of governance, and of course liberally borrowed from Sanjaya Baru's book. In contrast to what he has projected the Gandhi family as, Mr. Modi claims that the BJP is like a "family" and that he is a "team player." He does not believe in concentration of power, he says, even as he has consistently undermined almost all the senior leaders of the party, including L.K. Advani, Murli Manohar Joshi and Jaswant Singh. How many of us can recollect the names of any other cabinet minister in the Gujarat government? How many of us know that Mr. Modi kept 14 portfolios for himself, including Home, which perhaps is unprecedented in the history of post-independence politics? But all these are depicted as signs of a "strong and decisive" leader and someone who believes in hard work. Yet, the leader in question feigns complete ignorance when it comes to the 2002 riots. Mr. Modi campaigned hard against growing corruption in the Congress, even as he strongly supported the return of Yeddyurappa to the BJP and the candidature of Sriramulu in Karnataka, despite Sushma Swaraj's opposition.

Caste Issues

On caste, the BJP has claimed that it is moving beyond divisive caste politics — *Sab ka saath, Sab ka vikas* (Participation by all for development for all)," even as the entire campaign in Bihar is based on referring to Mr. Modi's the Other Backward Classes status. Mr. Modi himself claimed in Kerala that he belongs to the "Dalit family"; it is for this "family" that he wishes to do something if he takes the reins, he said. He shares the dais with Baba Ramdev, again a silent gesture towards combining OBC politics with Hindutva. Even as the BJP's manifesto does not mention its support for reservations and instead promises to move towards "equal opportunity," it believes that a Constitutional provision of reservations is mere "tokenism." Mr. Modi does not reveal which sub-caste he actually belongs to; instead he claims to represent all the poor in India. He is a "*chaiwallah* (tea seller)" who rose through sheer determination unlike the "*shehzada* (prince)" of the Congress.

Further Mr. Modi's campaign was singularly focused on propagating the "Gujarat model." This should have ideally led to an alternative policy frame taking centre-stage on his campaign trail, but this was not so. Not only was there no sustained debate on what these policies will be that will reproduce the magic of the Gujarat model elsewhere in India, but also that possibility was consciously avoided by delaying the release of the BJP's manifesto to the first day of polling — the message being that it is not "mere" policies on paper that matter but leadership. Thus, the repeated references to how Mr. Modi's popularity is higher than even that of the BJP is being repeated ad nauseam. Therefore, Mr. Modi does not find it difficult to not only replace the party but also the state and the nation. When he is criticised he makes a pitch for how "Gujarat *gaurav* " suffers. When he was asked recently to answer on the "snoopgate" controversy, he remarked that it has "shamed India globally." All this while claiming that democratic institutions have to be strengthened.

All this has been combined with a targeted strategy of nullifying any criticism against him by redirecting the same at his opponents. He launched the offensive against Nitish Kumar for being ambitious about becoming the Prime Minister, repeatedly criticised Chidambaram for being arrogant, and criticised Sonia Gandhi for appearing in an "advertisement" that was telecast as her message to the nation. The BJP also accused the Congress of being the "most communal party."

Finally, to all the uncomfortable questions he faced, Mr. Modi found answers. He said he was elected back three times in Gujarat and said "winning had become a habit," even as his own colleague in Madhya Pradesh achieved the same feat with much less controversial governance. The moot point is this: this does not seem to take away the sheen of the campaign or make it look hypocritical. How much of this has got to do with those planning his campaign trial and the media, and the willingness of the electorate to believe such performativity as a way of relating to and making sense of the spectacle called elections, is still an open question.

Published in *The Hindu*, May 8, 2014.

22

The Return of the Personality Cult

With crisis brewing in the Aam Aadmi Party and complaints of 'dictatorial traits' on the one hand, and the ascendance of the Modi-phenomenon on the other, one could ask if India has taken a turn towards a personality-centred politics? While we continue to take pride in democracy, we seem to be gradually slipping into a morass that collectively pushes us towards the myth that strong personalities can perform magic in overcoming the hurdles that we routinely face. There are various reasons that have led to this fructifying of our overt admiration and utter dependence on hero-worship as the last resort and last ray of hope.

India has always claimed strong leaders from Jawaharlal Nehru to Sardar Vallabbhai Patel to Indira Gandhi. However, over a period of time strong personalities have emerged primarily by undermining institutions. They appear as an alternative to the despondency and desperation created by institutional decay. Individual leaders seem to express strong leadership qualities only when institutions and accompanying procedures are weakened. This was evident in the 1970s with Mrs. Gandhi's undermining of internal democracy within the Congress. Chief Ministers were handpicked by the 'high command' while she made an open proclamation for a more committed judiciary and bureaucracy as a manner of demonstrating her control over the 'system'. She was lauded as 'Durga' for her role in liberating Bangladesh. Congress won elections based exclusively on her campaigns and she made it a point to demonstrate that she could win elections even from the South when she contested from Medak in Andhra Pradesh (although this was considered to be a 'safe seat'). The parallel in the strategy with Modi contesting from Varanasi cannot be missed. The slogan then was 'India is Indira, Indira is India'. Today, it has been scaled up, moving beyond the nation into a conflation with the 'all mighty' himself—'*Har Har Modi, Ghar Ghar Modi*'. The contest now is over the Central Bureau of Investigation—you either control it or claim to be a victim of its vindictive campaign. We refuse to believe that there can be anything like a transparent investigation, or a fair trial. In expanding the personality cult, more institutions will have to succumb to this phenomenon, including the Election Commission of India, the hints of which we already have seen in the recently concluded general elections.

Even those political practices that we can otherwise consider to be progressive and contributing towards the democratic well-being of our institutions can, willy-nilly, aid this process of undermining them altogether and leaving the space to be occupied by 'strong', 'decisive' and 'incorruptible' individuals. Consider the promulgation of the Right to Information Act (RTI): rather than empowering the vulnerable, it has instead contributed more robustly towards exposing public institutions and the decay within them, unsparing even of the legislature, executive and the judiciary. It has inadvertently contributed to the dominant mood of our times, which is that 'everyone is corrupt', except for the corporate world that does not come under the scrutiny of the RTI at all. The public role of the state inversely begins to look like a private institution, owned and 'managed' by few, while the private or corporate sector begins to assume the proportions of a public institution with their contribution to the nation's growth, its apparently selfless philanthropic activities, its investment in education and health, and the discourse generated about employment 'for all'. This, even as the deaths of RTI activists has now become a regular news feature.

In a similar vein, one the major protest movements in India in recent times, the one against corruption, has served to further increase popular disillusionment with political institutions. Anna Hazare's soap opera combined a rich participatory ethos with a drive for centralisation of power in the single institution of the *lokpal* (citizen-ombudsman), managed by 'five wise men'. The all-pervasive corruption in the system can apparently only be arrested by an all-powerful Lokpal. In this imagining, democracy and diversity are considered a hindrance to accountability and the efficient functioning of institutions. Representation is suspect, since it is bought with votes and liquor. Thus, politics and politicians can be considered dispensable (they can be 'recalled') as long as there is a strong centre of power, managed by those 'above' the corruptibility of the representative process, just as if in a Bollywood movie. Self-righteous claims provide the necessary justification for 'righteous lawlessness'. How far in time can it be then that 'five wise men' are replaced with one wise, strong and decisive superhero?

Neoliberal reforms of the last two decades have also contributed liberally to the resurgence of personality-based politics in India. The facelessness of the model with transnational capital flows makes it difficult to find the source of political and economic processes. For those living in rural hinterlands, the agrarian crisis is evident but the reasons are not as clear. Even the upwardly mobile professional classes and middle classes are experiencing mobility *with* uncertainty. The emergent 'risk society' grows and spreads with the withdrawal of social security measures, 'hire and fire' policy frames, voluntary retirement schemes, and the retrenchment, contractualisation and informalisation of employment. This is markedly different from the European experience where middle classes had a stake in democratic processes, in stable and autonomous intermediary institutions as a sustainable basis for democracy, which in turn delivered assured social security. Earlier the UPA regime had two power centres: it was driven by a division of labour where the Gandhi family stood for welfare and a human face made of the social security net, while Manmohan Singh and the Planning Commission were considered the motors of growth. While the Gandhi's won the elections for the Congress, the Manmohan-Montek team took care of the economy. The tussle between the two, however, created confusion and became susceptible to 'policy paralysis'. Now, we have moved to a model where a single individual has struck it out to claim responsibility for bringing back a robust economy, employment and a fast-paced urbanisation. He has promised stability which he earlier suggested could be achieved through calls for 'compulsory voting'. More recently this was reinforced by the rather 'nationalistic' suggestion made by Sri Sri Ravishanker to prohibit regional parties from contesting for elections to the Lok Sabha, in order to avoid the 'mess' of coalitions. In times that are bleak and opaque, the brevity and finiteness of an individual figure holds clarity and has created enthusiasm in the public imagination. If in the process institutions are weakened, who should be worried?

Published in *The Himal*, June 24, 2014.

23

The Modi Wave: Who is a Good Leader?

After the rather dismal performance of the Congress in the general elections and being reduced to a paltry sum of 44 seats in the Parliament, and struggling to find ways of retaining the post of the leader of the opposition, the question that is silently doing the rounds is if there is a future for the Congress as a formidable political party? Or will it gradually disintegrate into smaller political units and witness a series of splits. The dilemma seems to be that Congress cannot hold together as a party without the Gandhi family but has also seemingly hit a roadblock with Rahul Gandhi at the helm as its leader. The Congress is in a quandary to find a way out of this quagmire. The problem that seems to have some degree of general agreement is that Rahul Gandhi is a weak leader. Even Mr. Natwar Singh in his recent revelations has observed that Rahul Gandhi does not have enough 'fire in his belly' and that he is only a 'part-time politician'. The general complaint is he does not come across as strong willed. He does not come across as someone committed full-time 24/7 to politics and managing his party. What then is the subterranean idea of a good leader in Indian politics?

The dilemma is on the one hand the popular perception of a good leader is someone who comes across as being decisive, clear-minded and takes decisions without really dithering or giving in to the vagaries of political uncertainties, while on the other we also wish that leaders should be more amenable to public opinion, should be approachable, accountable, affable and therefore should respect intra-party democracy, and introduce elections within the political party. Can these two really go together? The dilemmas of popular perceptions that drive our opinion has been at the heart of how political leaders have managed their parties and the way they come to project themselves at large. Indira Gandhi was on the one hand lauded for her strong, and even authoritarian personality, and was deemed as 'Durga' but she was also chastised for undermining inner party democracy, and for initiating a process of de-institutionalisation and making demands for a 'committed judiciary' that finally landed Indian democracy in the crisis of the Emergency in 1975. This tension and friction between rather opposed imaginations of leadership is a continuing thread of Indian politics and democracy. The story is very similar with what happened to Mr. Arvind Kejriwal, who was touted as an honest, and an approachable leader, and one who cared for public opinion, but was also criticised for holding a dharna on the streets and doing a sit-in as the chief minister of Delhi. The general opinion then was that a leader, cannot bring down the prestige- *garima-* of an official position by sitting on the streets as a 'commoner', he needs to maintain dignity that comes from a distance. Here looking approachable is no longer perceived to be an act of bringing power closer to the common citizen but as a violation of sense of self as a citizen. Kejriwal himself had agreed that what he did came as a 'cultural shock' to the aam aadmi in Delhi and elsewhere. It is in fact this act of his that raised serious doubts in the minds of the common citizen whether he is fit to rule, and whether he has the ability to govern.

Similarly, a good leader in India, as is perceived, cannot be a 'part-time' politician, he has to be a professional, and committed round the clock busy with the machinations of party and government. Added to this is the idea that a good and a strong leader is one who is an ascetic, and believes in renouncing his personal and private pursuits for the larger cause of the nation. By this logic, therefore those without a family are often, ipso facto, considered to be honest leaders. Power has to be managed with a single-minded pursuit and without personal attachments. This is the gift of Gandhian imagination of *brahmacharya, meaning* celibacy in the immediate sense but also a sense of detachment, in the broader sense. It is therefore more than a coincidence that those considered as 'strong leaders' of

India, led by Mr. Modi, including Mamta Banerjee, Jayalalitha, Navin Patnaik, and Mayawathi, are those who fit this bill. They pursue power single-mindedly and full-time, and never display private emotions. In contrast to all of this is the way Rahul Gandhi comes across as someone who is affable and innocuous. He does not have the 'sting' to carry out the machinations necessary to carry out 'party activities' and gain 'control' of the party. He does not hesitate to show his private emotions or family ties with his mother and sister. He does not look obsessed, therefore he also does not seem 'committed'. He is a 'son' and not someone who is 'strong' enough to stand above personal emotions, since he also looks vulnerable to being bogged down by personal incidents in his life of losing his grandmother and his father. The idea of power, it appears like, cannot go with a human sensibility. There is a deep discomfort with the idea of the private, the everyday and with being ordinary. It has to be larger than life, and masculine; that is the only way you gain the 'respect' of the fellow partymen and also the cadre. In this mode of imagining, the leader cannot or should not ever face dissent and difference of opinion, for these are not considered as healthy democratic practices but signs of weakness and disrespect.

Finally, a leader cannot afford to retire and pursue other interests. This is generally perceived to be as someone who has 'given up', the lust for life. This cuts across the Left and the Right. It is therefore that in the Left parties, leaders don't retire, they simply die as 'Communists'. Notions of leisure raise serious doubts on one's commitment. There is a serious problem for those who lead an active public life to retreat into the anonymity of the private. This is something specific to the culture of our nation. Nelson Mandela who led a tireless public life as part of the anti-apartheid struggle very seamlessly slipped into a quiet private life. Even Mr. Goerge Bush preferred to pursue painting, after a rather 'eventful' two-terms as the president of the United States. It therefore came as a relief, when Mr. Chidambaram declared his interest to pursue his other interests to read and write, and seek retirement, but he was never a popular, 'mass leader', who had to manage a burgeoning political party. We seem to love the idea of a democratic leader in the abstract but when it takes a more concrete shape, he faces rejection; for a bit of ego in each one of us is hurt.

24

Modi and Gandhi

The fact that Mr. Modi and Gandhi are both from Gujarat is insufficient to explain Modi's new found love for Gandhi. The troubled relations that the RSS has had with Gandhi in the past makes it even more intriguing. Modi of late has been often asking in his public meetings, including the one he delivered at Madison Square in the United States that Gandhi has got us freedom from the yoke of British rule, what have we given Gandhi in return? During the high decibel campaign days of general elections the focus was on Sardar Patel, to deride the Nehruvian legacy, and interestingly during the time of governance, Modi has preferred to revert to Gandhi, putting Patel and the project of building a massive statue for the *'Loha Purush'* in Gujarat on the backburner. What will Gandhi bring to Modi's repertoire of political strategies? Is Gandhi and Gandhian philosophy being appropriated from the Congress, or is Gandhian philosophy being emptied of all its substantive meaning and being reduced to a symbol of cleanliness?

At the heart of Gandhian philosophy of bringing about radical social change was the strategy of drawing a separation between the social and the political domains. In other words, social change needs to be necessarily brought about independent of political mobilisation that often involves the language of antagonism, interests, and conflict. As part of the anti-colonial struggle, Gandhi reserved the political mobilisation, marked by mass mobilisation and non-cooperation against the British, while these were interspersed by periods of what was referred to as 'constructive work'. Constructive work, included issues such as cleanliness, fight against untouchability, among others.

Here, the change was sought not through mass mobilisation and non-cooperation but by mutual cooperation and understanding in the social domain. Therefore Gandhi offered the ideas of Trusteeship to address economic inequalities, idea of 'change of heart' theory to bring about changes in the caste hierarchy, and taking up programmes to clean public toilets in Dalit (then Harijan) colonies in order to de-stigmatise the profession of scavenging and also dignifying manual labour. The social was the domain of unity and consensus, while political was the domain of conflict; social was spiritual, while political was more material; social taught the art of cooperation, accommodation, obligation, duty and responsibility, while political was the domain of resistance and assertion (even if it was through 'passive resistance'). This then was the paradox of the Gandhian strategy of bringing about social change through the 'politics of accommodation', which is what Francine Frankle refers to as the 'Gradual Revolution'. It is this separation between the social and the political, where the social stands above the 'bickering' of the everyday politics that Modi has much to gain from in launching the *Swachh Bharat Abhiyan*, and why the ruling elite time and again feel compelled and convenient to invoke Gandhi.

The campaign for cleanliness is precisely to bring back this mode of creating the wedge between the social and the political. Cleanliness marks an impending need to bring a 'social' change in making Indian towns and cities clean. This cannot be brought about, as the campaign would have us believe, through the language of politics and political mobilisation, but together by realising mutual responsibilities and duties. Further, cleaning cannot be the responsibility of the state alone but needs voluntary participation of the citizens, no point blaming the state and government for 'everything' without realising one's own role in it. In doing this, Mr. Modi seeks to turn the gaze onto one's own society and community, rather than focusing and expecting 'everything' from the government. In laying the blame on the government, one could be projected as being irresponsible, because Gandhi had said 'be the change that you want to see in the world'. If we have our limitations, then the government for sure will also have its own limitations and compulsions. This needs empathy, and not criticism, in order to understand if things are not being delivered, as promised.

Cleaning as a symbol is also important for the caste connotations it carries. Mr. Modi began the cleaning process from a Balmiki colony in Delhi, again a classical Gandhian posturing, which not only dignifies the act of sweeping but also serves as a reminder that it is not the responsibility of karamcharis alone to keep the public spaces clean. In demanding that it is the sole responsibility of the karamcharis, one might unwittingly thrust the language of sweeping belonging to specific caste groups, and therefore it is more prudent to accept that it is a shared responsibility rather than that of karamcharis, even if they are state employees in Municipal corporations. Gandhi was the genius of symbolism during the anti-colonial struggle. He realised that one way to create a sense of togetherness in a society that was deeply divided was to create symbols that are relevant in the everyday sense across class and caste. Cleanliness is a similar kind of everyday practice that Modi wishes to flag off as a symbol of a resurgent India, the new India that has arrived on the global map, which can be understood by everyone—'125 crore Indians'—across board.

Finally, Modi's strategy of sending out invitations to personalities from the filmdom, sports and even to politicians like Shashi Tharoor of the Congress is to drive home the point that this is 'above politics'. The strategy has always been to subsume, supplant and contain the messy terrain of the political with the sanitised consent of the social, but to what effect this time around, we will only know by 2019, not only because it is the year of Gandhi's 150th anniversary by when the clean India campaign has to achieve its target but also it is the year for the next general elections.

Published in *Deccan Herald*, October 18, 2014.

Left in India

25

Left Parties: Pragmatic or Dogmatic?

In 2004 when UPA-I came into existence the Left parties played a pivotal role in deciding the content of the Common Minimum Programme and pushing social welfare policies, at the height of economic reforms. In fact, it was this continuous check of the Left Front with their outside support to the government that Congress promulgated the much acclaimed MGNREGA that literally catapulted it back into power in 2009. However, with UPA-II the Left did not do so well electorally compared to its previous tally of 60 MPs in 2004, while Congress on its own managed to get 206 MPs. The Left parties did not support the UPA-II, and story now seems to be very different as we are headed towards the General Elections, 2014, with neither the Left nor the Congress keeping good health. While the electoral prospects of the Congress look rather bleak, the Left parties have hardly made their presence felt. Is the Indian Left headed towards a terminal decline?

The declining electoral presence and prospects of the Left parties is representative of deeper economic and political changes that have come about in the last couple of decades. These changes have multiplied the complexity of the challenge that the Left always faced on the social and electoral front, but this time around the Left seems ill-prepared in re-inventing itself. India is one of the few countries of this size in the world that has a massive informal sector, accounting for 84.7% of the jobs in the economy. The increasing informalisation of the economy has posed a grave challenge to the conventional trade union modes of mobilisation and organising the work force that formed the traditional base of the Left parties. The new kind of

'Footloose labour' has no permanent firm or a regular employee. They are mostly self-employed and continue to migrate in search of work, making it difficult to mobilise them on any sustainable basis. Similarly, on the rural front the traditional farmer's movement has rearticulated itself along the lines of caste politics that is reflected in the rise of the politics of the OBCs that aspire not for better returns in agriculture but what they perceive to be upward mobility with an opportunity to shift to the urban centres with secured employment. This phenomenon of being mobilised along caste lines is occurring alongside de-mobilisation along the traditional class-lines in spite of the growing agrarian crisis in many states, resulting in a spate of farmer's suicides. It is clear that beyond a level of distress the subaltern cannot be mobilised into traditional protest forms. Neoliberal economic reforms has not only dispossessed the rural poor but also disarmed them into submission. While CPI has played an active role in waging various struggles, including those against POSCO in Odisha, they have remained utterly localised and the Left parties themselves have failed in linking them to other struggles at the national level.

The debate in India has shifted from land reforms, a traditional slogan of the Left parties, to land acquisition. Today it is about protecting the land that the subaltern possesses, and not about 'land to the tiller'. The debate has moved from redistribution to maximisation of wealth, as a purported viable strategy to even benefit the poor. Who has then occupied the streets that have been vacated by the subaltern? The streets have been taken over by an unlikely social class—the urban middle classes. It is today the middle classes that have taken to street protest politics—conjuring, what Saskia Sassan refers to as the 'global street', all across the world from the Occupy movement in New York to the Arab Spring in Egypt- around the issues of corruption, violence against women and crime. It is the young among the middle classes that have become the new symbol of protest with their indomitable candle light marches. Street protests that have remained for long an inspiring transformative spectacle of the left politics are today the weapon of the privileged middle classes that have never constituted the social base of the Left parties. As the middle classes have occupied the imagination of a resurgent nation, it has also eclipsed the presence of the Left parties.

On the electoral front too the Left parties have been caught unaware of the fast-paced changes that have engulfed it with the increasing 'mediatisation of politics'. The Left continues to operate along with its old methods based on Party programme and policy that are not easily amenable to the demands of mediatisation. In a recent interview Prakash Karat referring to the difference with AAP's strategy of fighting corruption suggested that, 'its not just a question of targeting some individuals; it's a question of policy'. While symbolism can be without substance, but substance without symbols can be synthetic. In representative democracies, especially of the size and diversity of India, symbols and popular perception are of immense significance. This also adds a further complexity where issues that are pertinent in terms of economy and sovereignty of the nation, need not necessarily be electorally viable. This was precisely the point that it is perhaps the Left parties alone that could have withdrawn their support on an issue such as the Indo-nuclear deal in 2008 that meant little in much of rural hinterlands and in gaining electoral returns. But if such issues are considered important, it is pertinent to ask how does one then convert them into an electorally viable strategy? Ideologically oriented parties will always face the dilemma of how much to change and compromise in terms of the vagaries of popular democracy, unlike parties such as AAP which can one day fight Ambani and on another day can declare to CII, as Arvind Kejriwal did that 'government has no business of being in business'. He In fact declared that AAP has nothing against capitalism. It could protest against violence against women by doing a sit-in one day and declare Khap Panchayats as cultural organisations on another sunny day. This pragmatism in AAP's own self-understanding is representative of its open-minded, unscripted and creative political potential. In opposition to AAP's pragmatism is the thin line between ideological commitment and rugged dogmatism of the Left parties. The choice between pragmatism and dogmatism is one that has consistently bogged down the Left parties.

Finally, in the run up to the 2014 General Elections, the Left has desperately yet again attempted its old fashioned method of cobbling up a third front, as an alternative to both Congress and the BJP. Mostly, the third Front's were forged either against the corruption of Congress or the communal politics of the BJP. It was a Front forged by exclusion, in other words it was more important who was being excluded rather than what is being included. In today's so-called post-ideological scenario where from Ram Vilas Paswan to M.J.Akbar have found their own reasons to join the Modi bandwagon, the Left parties really have no clue how to constitute an alternative Front. Ideally they should have attempted to project an alternative social democratic and pro-welfare agenda as the basis for bringing various regional parties together. By abdicating common and alternative agenda as the viable basis for the Third Front, the Left parties too have followed suit the number game. For instance, in Andhra Pradesh, the Left parties lead the farmer's agitation against Telugu Desam Party for increasing the electricity tariff as part of the World Bank initiated changes but decided to enter into an alliance with the same party in the 2009 Assembly elections. The wedge between Left parties' political vision and electoral calculations has also pushed them into what looks like a serious crisis in the clarity of their thought and choices they are making. Similarly, Left parties that rejected the offer of making Jyoti Basu the Prime Minister in 1996, are today being turned away from the doorstep of AIADMK, this indeed makes for a rather traumatized picture of what is left of the Left. Whether the current brand of octogenarians and septuagenarians can find one last opportunity to seriously introspect the orientation and direction that Left parties need to take in times to come, is indeed a 'million dollar' question.

Published in the *Economic and Political Weekly* (Web Exclusives)
Vol. XLIX, No. 17, April 26, 2014.

26

Maoists and the Official Marxists

Book review of Maoism: A Critique from the Left *edited by Presenjit Bose (Leftword, Delhi, 2010).*

One of the imperatives of transformative politics aiming for radical change has been to overcome the insurmountable complexity of pursuing praxis with a singularity of purpose, and yet not abandon critical enquiring into the philosophical presuppositions guiding that practice, as much as contributing to the philosophy itself. Communist politics has more often than not fallen victim to this condition, preferring to take the soft option of perpetuating the enduring gap. The reasons for such a durable disconnect could be many. It could be due to the kind of (macro) structural issues that they have been grappling with, which demand a certain degree of centralisation and singularity of practice that can ill-afford the privilege of keeping *strategies* open-ended; It could also be, more specific to the Indian reality, due to the embedded nature of caste relations (and the accompanying caste-psyche) that demands hierarchy, segregated and enclosed-practices that replicate themselves *in* and *through* the very political mode one is operating in. For instance, there seem to be uncanny parallels between the ways the Communist parties repeat the dictums of Mao and Lenin, and the rhetoric and performative aspects of a *bhajan* (not to miss that upper-castes for long have dominated the leadership of these political groups), or the compulsion of being 'pure' (the eternal search for 'pure' subjectivity) that gets expressed in being 'scientific' or following *the* 'correct line' (that is claimed by few and known to none). But then, it could well be due to the sheer complexity involved in relating the abstract to the concrete. As Marx observes in *Grundrisse,* 'It would seem right to start with the real and concrete, with the actual presupposition, e.g. in political economy to start with the population... Closer consideration shows, however, that this is wrong. Population is an abstraction if, for instance, one disregards the classes of which it is composed. These classes in turn remain an empty phrase if one does not know the elements on which they are based, e.g. wage labour, capital, etc. From there it would be necessary to make a return journey until one finally arrived once more at population, which this time would be not a chaotic conception of a whole, but a rich totality of many determinations and relations'[1]. Consider, for instance, the strangeness of the idea of individual, which is the most real-concrete category but sociologically it could be a very abstract idea bereft of a social location. All these factors, along with the more visible phenomenon of the brutal nature of state repression on militant struggles in India has only made the task all that more difficult.

How should Communist politics then reinvent itself? This crisis in the search for alternatives, due to the debilitating arrest of the flow between creative theory and resolute practice, is in the pressing need of raising new questions—as Zapatistas say 'asking we walk'. Rather than an attempt to look for new signposts that can give us credible clues to come out of the impasse, the book under review is squarely part of this perpetuating crisis. It only makes it graver when the essays are written by those involved in the vocation of active politics, in this case while one of the essays is written by P.M.S. Grewal, Secretary of the Delhi State Committee of the CPM, the other by Nilotpal Basu, member of the Central Secretariat of the same party.

One of the central propositions on which the book and its critique of the Maoists in India is based is the idea that we need to chalk out 'our' own Indian strategy rather than 'relying upon (such) imported know-how to make revolution and trying to blindly imitate it'(p.15). This agenda is set by the editor of the volume and is repeated by both the afore-mentioned contributors. It is ironical that the authors are critical of Maoists for blindly imitating the Chinese revolution, while the authenticity of their own positions is validated by verbatim quotes from Lenin! For instance, Grewal is critical of Maoists for poll boycott and their mistaken idea that the situation in India is ripe for revolution because 'keeping the rich experience of the Russian Revolution in mind, Lenin had in his 1920 work *Left Wing Communism, An Infantile Disorder*, outlined certain features of a situation ripe for revolution...Those who claim that a revolutionary situation, even remotely similar to the one described above exists in India today obviously have no touch with reality' (p.42). Grewal does not think it is necessary to raise the issue as to why should the situation be similar to Russia, if it isn't necessary with regard to China. He, instead, further argues that the 'Bolsheviks participated in elections to the bourgeois Parliament in Russia or the Constituent Assembly...By the Maoist logic, however, Lenin and the Bolshevik Party should be accused of revisionism!' (Ibid). Grewal then invites Maoists to learn from the failures of the militant struggles in Peru and Philippines, and the shift to the parliamentary politics in Nepal. The obvious contradiction in purpose and methods adopted is linked to the fact that all analysis is in the 'last instance' justifiably a form of propaganda. This point is only further reinforced in the way various points are repeated in both the essays by the office-bearers of the CPM. This mode of 'analysing' issues seem to have close links with the centrality of state power in the Communist strategy, where everything one does need to be part of a cumulative process that converges on a central point. This is not to neglect state power but to be conscious of the possibility of being *statised* in your modes of operation in course of negotiating with it. Thinking and acting like a state can well happen being out of state power.

The authors could have instead raised the more important question in relation to the debate between Parliamentary form versus armed struggle, for instance, as to growing stalemate and the inability to bring transformation, or even stalling the policies of the rulers, either through armed struggle or through elections. It is also obvious that those Communist parties participating in elections have not made a dramatic impact in blocking the wanton spread of neoliberalism. There have been, at best, partial and sporadic successes by struggles of all hues. How then can radical protest politics come out of this deadlock? What could be the new modes of protest that need to be invented? Questions and answers that might go beyond the existing perceptions, and the compulsion of claiming to know the 'correct strategy for revolution'. It wouldn't be perhaps inappropriate to recollect D.D.Kosambi's caution that 'Marxism is a method of thinking and not a substitute to thinking'.

NOTES

1. Karl Marx, Grundrisse, in *Collected Works* (Volume 28) (Progress Publishers, Moscow, 1986, p. 37).

Published in the *Book Review,* September 9, 2010.

27

Reconstructing Marxism: The Thompsonian Frame

Notwithstanding the constraints of space and obvious limitations in analysing the anthology of Thompson' s writings, Bhupendra Yadav, in his article 'E.P. Thompson: Scholar, Polemicist and Pacifist' *(Social Scientist,* Vol. 26, Nos. 11-12, November-December 1997), has not brought into relief some of the most significant and long lasting theoretical contributions of EPT. EPT has not only influenced history writing in a decisive way (for instance, his writings precursors 'Subaltern Studies' tradition), but also the course of development and direction of Marxist theory. It is, perhaps, therefore imperative to comprehend EPT more as a 'Marxist' than in de-ideologised terms such as a 'scholar' or 'polemicist' .

One of the most fundamental reformulations of EPT that has decisively determined the 'foundations' and thereby the direction of Marxist theory, is his rejection of the base—superstructure model. He argued that historical materialism has to be founded not on a segregated notion of reality, represented in the base-superstructure model, but on the model of organic totality as represented in the dictum 'social being determines social consciousness' . According to EPT, most of the mechanistic and teleological formulations of history and social processes by Marxists, had their roots in the base-superstructure metaphor. He in fact argued that Marx, in a sense, was himself responsible for reductionist interpretations and the later 'crisis of Marxism'.

According to Thompson, Marx's work evolved in two distinct phases. First was the *'Grundrisse Phase'* where he developed a static, anti historical structure because he "proposed that it was possible not only to identify particular activities as 'economic' but to isolate these as special field of study from other activities (political, religious, legal, moral, cultural, etc)."[1] Such a method of study, where economy (or capital to be more specific) is an operative category which laws its own development (where impingement of politics or law upon economic activity is seen as an improper interference with natural economic process), cannot capture the whole society or real historical process because the later comprises of "many activities and relations (of power of consciousness, sexual, cultural and normative) which are not the concern of political economy and which have been defined out of political economy."[2] According to Thompson only that historical materialism which could bring all activities and relations within a coherent view could capture the imbricated social process indissolubly linked in human practice.

However, Marx in his *Capital* volumes seems to have provided this coherent view with his attempt to comprehend capital as a social relation and not an isolated economic category. Capitalist production is fundamentally a social relation based on the disposition of power which enables it to reproduce its conditions of existence and therefore forms the indissoluble part of the production process itself, i.e. capitalist production cannot be visualised without these social relations.

In other words, Thompson was critical of all Marxists who "adopted modes of analysis which, explicitly treat the economic base and the legal, political and ideological superstructure which reflect or correspond to it as a qualitatively different more or less enclosed and regionally separated spheres."[3] Such epistemological distinctions convert into ontological segregations, thereby capturing the historical process not at the moment of unitary coexistence of various human activities within a single material life but in terms of artificial discontinuities. In other words, what is imperative to comprehend is that the economic base is not just neglected in and maintained by certain superstructural institutions, but that the 'productive base itself exists in the shape of social, juridical and political forms'.

E.P. Thompson seems to have made a distinction benveen 'economic base' and the 'material base' as used byMarx. Marx almost always uses the word 'material,' for instance 'the material forces of production', 'the material transformation of the economic conditions' implying a distinction between 'material transformation' and 'economic conditions'.[4] 'Material' referred to the fundamental conditions of human production both economic and non-economic. The base could thus include, the natural environment, human hereditary endowment, interaction of man and nature was among the 'material forces of production', organisation of the work process and division of labour among the vvorking personnel, education was involved in the production of the most important of all commodities—labour power, law, rights and policy are in certain respects superstructural and in other respects basic (for instance, governing institutions have continuously intervened in the economic system), in a healthy society art and aesthetic impulse occupy an important place in the base.[5]

EPT therefore argues that historical process should be studied v.ith reference to the determination of 'material base' rather than just 'economic' instance within it. For this, it is important to capture various 'structures' (mode of production, production relations, etc) as operative historical principles—the way they occur in real history—rather than as abstract structures with pre-given lavs. For this purpose, "the analogy of basis and superstructure is radically defective. It cannot be repaired. It has an in-built tendency to lead the mind towards reductionism or a vulgar economic determinism, by sorting out human activities and attributes and placing some (as law, the arts, religion, morality) in a superstructure others (as technology, economic, applied sciences) in a basis, and leaving yet others (as linguistics, work discipline) to float unhappily in between".[6]

Now if production relations or mode of production itself is expressed simultaneously in economic, political, legal and cultural relations, what happens to the proposition that 'economic' determination is central to Marxist theory? It is important to note that Thompson does not intend to conflate production relations with all social relations in a social formation. "A distinction must be drawn between the principle that relations of production are all relations between people in a class society, that base is also and at the same time superstructure and Thompson's own very different proposition,"[7] where he is primarily arguing that products of social activity, the forms of social interaction produced by men, themselves become material forces as much as natural givens (such as technology).

Similarly, in order to protect the specificity of 'production' and its determination, EPT seems to suggest the necessity "to distinguish between juridical-political forms tnat are the constituents of productive relations and those that are more distant from, or external to these relations—even if there are no sharp discontinuities between them."[8]

To put it in the base-superstructure language, we need to distinguish the 'basic' and 'superstructural' juridical-political and cultural attributes of the productive system.

Though the organic totality model of EPT overcame the reductionist propositions of the base-superstructure model, it had to face its own challenges from both Marxist and non-Marxist scholars.

One of the most pertinent questions that Thompson had to problematise, "With reference to his organic totality model, was the dichotomy betvveen social relations that constitute and correspond to economy and those material relations that are located at a distance. In what proper sense did this relation constitute an 'integrated social reality' or a 'totality' , as he claimed?

Thompson recognised this problematic domain, for any theory interested in arguing for an integrated social reality. "These two reservations—as to the complexity of the 'correspondence' and as to its significance—are so severe as to call in question the effectivity of Marx's general notions. Very few of the critically-significant problems which we confront in our actual lives appear to be directly and causally implicated in this field of correspondence: nationalism, racism, sexual oppression, fascism and Stalinism itself are certainly not removed from this field (for the pressure of class antagonisms and class ideologies can be felt in all), but equally certainly they cannot be seen as 'developed forms of the fundamental relation of production,' they are forms in their own right, and for their analysis we require a new set of terms."[9]

Thompson believes that the problem of 'correspondence' cannot be conceptualised in terms of structures interacting as enclosed domains "With an apriori logic of absolute determination. On the contrary, it can be understood only in terms of constitutent 'human practice' based on 'experience' i.e. various social structures in a totality correspond because they are the various activities of human beings "Within a unitary material life. In other words, human agency mediates the relation various structures and transmutes them into a 'process.' Human agents are born into given structures, they comprehend them through experience in their consciousness and then decide to deal "With them in a multi-fold manner. This common human 'experience (of structures as class experiences in a class based society) is the mode through which they correspond. "Kinship, custom, the invisible and visible rules of social regulation, hegemony and difference, symbolic forms of domination and of resistance, religious faith and millenarial impulses, manners and ideologies—all of which, in their sum, comprise the genetics of the whole historical process, all of them joined at a certain point in common human experience which itself (as distinctive class experiences) exerts its pressure on the sum."[10]

Thus, EPT opened the search for the micro-foundations of Marxist theory.He argued that individual and his needs and cherished concerns (cultural, sexual, normative, etc) are as important, to comprehend both 'correspondence' and 'motion' in historical process, as the study of over-arching structures (such as mode of production). It is only in their constitute and dialectical relation that clues to comprehend the 'integrated social realitf reside. It is only within this dialectical relation that concepts such as 'relative autonomy' and 'determination' should be defined and made sense of. 'Relative autonomy' of structures, therefore, is nothing but the dynamic and conscious human practice that operates in an open ended process. While, on the other hand 'determination' refers to 'setting of limits' . Economic determination sets the limits within which social process operates—specificities of this process are as aforesaid, determined by conscious human practice.

But did Thompson in reinvigorating micro-foundations connect them to the over-arching structural mutations? In other "Words, could he explain howthis micro-leveled human practice is linked to the shifting modes of production? Marxist scholars and historians of his period strongly believed that EPT failed in this. This failure of Thompson looms large in his foremost historical "Work, *The Making of the English Working Class.*"In the absence of any objective frame" Work laying dovvn the overall pattern of capital accumulation in these years, there is a little way of assessing how these processes are linked to human practice. Thus, "it is not the structural transformations—economic, political which Thompson invokes but rather their precipitates in the subjective experience cf those who lived through these terrible years."[11]

It is this unfinished project, of explaining the motion in the 'object' vis-a-vis the motion in the 'subject', within a totality or a systematic whole, that has opened new vistas far contemporary Marxist studies by Thompson's Marxism. It is only in the study of dynamic processes, events, phenomenon in their ovvn right, in a 'new set of terms' that we can justify the generic pronouncements of Marx, and establish socialism as a constitutive human way of life. Otherwise Marxist theory, according to EPT, would continue to make the 'theoricist' error of assuming that "there is some socialist mode of production within which some socialist relations of production are given, which will afford a categorical guarantee that some immanent socialist society will unfold itself, out of the womb of the mode of production itself."[12]

NOTES

1. Thompson, E.P. (1978). *Poverty of Theory*, Merlin Press, London, p. 60.
2. Ibid., p. 60.
3. Wood, E.M. (1981). 'Separation of the Economic and the Political in Capitalism', *New Left Review*, 127, p. 68.
4. Refer to Rader, Melvin. (1979). *Marx's Interpretation of History*, New York, OUP, for a detailed discussion of this point.
5. For an important but an alternative interpretation of Marx in terms of a distinction between 'material as economic' and 'social'

as non-economic, refer to Cohen, G.A. (1978). *Karl Marx's Theory of History,* Clarendon Press, Oxford.

6. Thompson, E.P. (1988). 'Folklore, Anthropology, and Social History', in *Indian Historical Review,* Vol. III, No. 2, January, p. 262.
7. Wood, E.M. 'Falling Through the Cracks: E.P. Thompson and the Debate on Base and Superstructure' in Kaye, H. and Maccle Land, K. (eds.) (1990). *E.P. Thompson: Critical Perspectives,* Policy Press, Cambridge, p. 139.
8. Wood, E.M. (1981). op. cit., p. 79.
9. Thompson, E.P. (1978). op. cit., pp. 160-161.
10. Ibid., p. 170.
11. Anderson, Perry (1981). *Arguments within English Marxism,* Verso, London, p. 34.
12. Thompson, E.P. (1978). op. cit., p. 161.

Published in the *Social Scientist,* 1998.

28

Marxism, Authoritariansism and People's Movements

Arun Patnaik's rejoinder (*EPW*, May 20, 1995) to K. Balagopal's article (*EPW*, January 7, 1995) rightly traces two important formulations of Balagopal that need to be critically rethought. However the limitation of Arun Patnaik's rejoinder stems from the attempts to understand the questions raised by Balagopal from the standpoint of classifical Marxism and he therefore fails to note that limitations lie not only in Balagopal's theorisation but also in classical Marxism itself. Similarly, while Balagopal slipped into idealism trying to comprehend the decisive turns in contemporary polity, Arun Patnaik makes no such effort. In a letter written to Dagobert Oppenheim (August 25, 1842), Marx insisted that "true theory must be developed and clarified within the concrete circumstances and in relation to existing conditions." It is therefore essential that the historical works of Marx and Engels have to be placed where they rightly belong, within the limits which they themselves assigned to them, in accordance with the circumstances of their publication.

Arun Patnaik points out the first limitation as Balagopal's emphasis on the role of the state in accomplishing a secular democratic polity. He, therefore, writes, "for both [Banerjee and Balagopal] in fact the unit of counter politics is the reorganised state power."

This decisive shift in Balagopal's arguments from tracing the agent of transformation in civil society (exploited classes, castes and social groups) to his faith in a democratised state as an agent of transformation is both nebulous and needs a thorough search for the reasons behind such a shift. The centrality of Balagopal's arguments is his attempt to search for an agent of transformation that can carry humankind to its cherished millennium. This search (and failure) is similar to the kind of search that Marx himself engaged in tracing an agent of revolution in civil society rejecting the Hegelian identification of the state as the transcendental principle.

I

Marx inherited the Hegelian perspective on civil society but he rejected the state and civil society as dual worlds with different rationale and logic as Hegel assumed. On the contrary, Marx argued that they are "the opposing poles of a single contradiction... civil society is the principal aspect of this contradiction" [Pierson 1986]. Lucio Colletti introducing the early works of Marx argues that in the critique Marx wrote of Hegel in 1843 there can be found "a clear statement of dependence of the state upon society, a critical analysis of parliamentarianism accompanied by a counter-theory of popular delegation and a perspective showing the need for ultimate suppression of the state itself". Politically the mature writings of Marx had little to add to this, concludes Colletti. Thus the base of the state remains civil society with all its economic divisions. Marx further argues that the principle which can transcend the particularities of civil life must be sought within the domain of the civil sphere itself. He therefore writes in *German Ideology:* "It is therefore evident that this civil society is the true hearth, the genuine stage of all history. The earlier concept of history can be seen as nonsence, for it disregarded the real relationships and limited itself to great historical and political events."

The thrust of such an argument is that a democratised state (for which Balagopal is pleading) cannot exist in a civil society whose relations and institutions are authoritarian. There is a strong structural linkage between the nature of state and civil society. In fact, struggles to democratise state power without concomitant struggles to democratise civil society are as futile as the struggles that restrict themselves to democratising civil society without fighting the authoritarian structures of an overarching state power (for instance, the failure of politics of reformism by Vinoba Bhave or the failure of the attempts to percolate the benefits to the poorer sections by voluntary organisations, etc). In fact, no world-view of tranformative politics is feasible without congnisance of this structural linkage.

Marxism made this dual change of state power and authoritarian structures of civil society central to its transformative politics. However, its conceptualisation of the definite process of democratising civil society (which includes changing the existing value-system and establishing revolutionary ideas) to a large extent remained unproblematised.

After Marx was convinced that not democracy but revolution was the way for fundamental transformation in history, he was in search of "a passive element, a material basis" necessary for that revolution. It is at this stage that Marx concluded that the proletariat as a class was the vehicle for revolution and was destined to assume the universal role that Hegel had misleadingly assigned to the bureaucracy. In the words of Marx, in his *Introduction to a Critique of Hegel's Philosophy of Right,* "...in the formation of a class with radical chains, a class in civil society that is not a class of civil society, of a social group that is the dissolution of all social groups, of a sphere that has a universal character because of its universal sufferings and lays claim to no particular right, because it is the object of no particular injustice in general. It is finally a sphere that cannot emancipate itself without emancipating these other spheres themselves. In a word, it is the complete redemption of humanity. This dissolution of society, as a particular class, is the proletariat..."

The assumption that is central to the entire Marxist conception of historical transformation is that of the proletariat "as society" which means that the poor lack the corruption of civil life because they lack property. Thus, the proletariat could not only emancipate itself but the whole of humanity. Such universality of the poor is romanticised by Marx because he does not problematise it. As Marcuse opines, "For Marx the fact that the poor are non-members of civil society means that they are spared from experiencing what I will call 'the disbenefits of social privilege' or the 'disadvantages in the advantages'. As Marx describes them in the debates 'the disadvantages of the advantages' concern the harmful effects of the private interest on people's moral character and consciousness. In other words, according to Marx it is only the members of civil society who experience the disadvantages of membership in a social order which is dominated by private interest."

This romanticised image of the class of proletariat is closely linked to his assumption of the inevitability of socialist society with the development of productive forces. As Neera Chandhoke writes in her recent book, *State and Civil Society,* "He [Marx] allots a particular property to a class on the basis of its location which is outside the civil society. He neither considers the political consciousness of this class as problematic nor does he consider that the poor may share the values of civil society reven if they do not share the material benefits of such a society." She further writes, "Marx pays little attention at this stage to the subjectivity of this class, though he examines the subjectivity of this class, though he examines the subjectivity of the rest of the classes in Germany. It almost seems that the proletariat does not need to develop subjectivity; it is already emancipated; therefore the emancipation of civil society by the this class is treated as umproblematic by Marx."

It is this hiatus in Marxism that Balagopal, with his immense experience as an activist in people's movements, tries to grapple with when he pleads for a fresh look at the familiar Marxist positions. He therefore writes, "The proletariat has nowhere exhibited the desire imputed to it by Marx to take charge of the affairs of humanity and rebuild its existence on the basis of communist collectivism."

However, in spite of tracing the limitations of the proletariat as a class and its inadequacy in bringing about a complete historical transformation, Balagopal makes no worthwhile breaks in theorising the transformative process. He makes no efforts to understand the historical role of social groups other than class and the historical indispensability of concrete struggles in extra-economic domains to complete the socialist project meaning the democratisation of civil society in its real sense (which would include Balagopal's idea of rejecting fanatical chauvinism of Hindutva as a value and therefore defeating it in all forms). On the contrary, Balagopal reverts to Hegelian idealist notions of the state transcending the particularities of civil society. He therefore argues that the motive of people's movements should be to ceaselessly strive to strenthen the one or the other wing of the state. Balagopal who attempted to clarify the dilemmas of Marxism in fact ends up in a dilemma of his own—on the one hand he is critical of the communist project that went the Stalinist way (if by that he means the excessive role of the state power) while on the other he himself pleads for a strong reorganised state to take up the project of democratising civil society.

However, considering the commitment that Balagopal himself has in mass struggles as a Human Rights activist, one can assume that he couldn't have possibly ignored the historical role of various social groups. What deterred Balagopal in resting his faith in such people's movements is perhaps clear when he writes, "history is witness to innumerable instances where those who have fought an authoritarianism that oppressed them have themselves turned authoritarian thereafter, for what they have fought is not oppression as such but the oppression of the other that has hurt their interests."

It is this replication of authoritariansim which convinced Balagopal that not just proletarian class struggle but no other material struggle can emancipate humankind from oppression. He not only rejects material struggles as the way for human emancipation but in fact rejects the historical possibility of such emancipation—a millennial victory. Once the struggles are rejected of opening the historical possibilities of human emancipation, it is only a matter of extending the logic to argue that autonomous moral psyche exists and its does not progress with concomitant struggles in the material realm. As Arun Patnaik writes, "it is no wonder that Balagopal who has been in the midst of this chaos over the last two decades responds partly like a common being terrorised by the self-arrogating discourses of liberation and seeks solace in the moral domain of love, compassion and tolerance for each other." But Arun Patnaik leaves the argument here without making an effort to understand this perpetual dischotomy of people's movements which in spite of being democratic and emancipatory in their goals are authoritarian and sectarian in their mode of achieving those goals.

II

Marx writes in *German Ideology*, "the thoughts of the dominant class are also in every age the dominant thoughts. In other words, the dominant material power of society is also its dominant spiritual power. The class that disposes of the means of material production disposes, by the same token, of those of intellectual production, so that generally speaking the thoughts of those who are deprived of the means of intellectual production are suppressed thoughts. And the dominant thoughts are themselves only the idealised expression of the dominant material relationships: they are those relationships seen in the form of ideas; they express all that makes a class a dominant class, they are in fact the idea of that domination."

It is this 'idea of domination' that becomes the fabric of civil society and therefore the existing relations and institutions of civil society such as caste, private property, family, religion, educational centres replicate authoritariansim in various forms. Authoritarianism as a value system not only replicates but also reinforces itself. Movements such as the religious reform movements and movements that sought to destroy practices which created deplorable conditions for women were never successful in achieving their goals because an attack on one form of authoritarianism separating it from all other coexisting forms of authoritarianism would not obliterate authoritarianism as a value-system. For instance, as Harbans Mukhia observes, patriarchal values reinforce communal sentiments of a society. He writes ('Communal Violence and Transmutation of Identities', *EPW*, June 10, 1995: "In her [Sadhvi Ritambhara's] speeches one dominant rhetoric is 'impotene' challenging the 'manhood' of those who would not attack and kill Muslims in riots—a challenge that becomes doubly inflammatory when thrown in public by a young lady."

It is in this civil society, which replicates authoritarianism in various forms, that people's movements are situated. They unconsciously become part of the dominant value-system and in spite of lighting against it they also replicate it. Therefore one need not be surprised when Naxalite leaders in Praja courts confer medieval punishments on the accused, such as tonsuring heads, chopping off hands, etc. This in itself creates a historical necessity of units of counter-politics against authoritarian values in all forms, of which agrarian struggles are but one such unit. Without understanding the necessity of such heterogeneous struggles and necessary linkages between them one cannot but assume psychoanalysis (where one might trace consequences of an event and not causal linkages) as the saviour.

Balagopal's article in spite of starting on the right note ends up as neo-liberal rhetoric because it fails to understand contemporary politics as assertions by plural social groups which are as indispensable as the historical role of proletariat. It is therefore essential to go beyond the Marxist understanding of transformation. Both the goals that are central to the Marxist understanding of transformation, i.e. of gaining political power by the proletariat and abolition of private property, in themselves cannot be the millennial victory. Emancipation of women must certainly go beyond abolition of private proverty as the basis of family. Similarly the proletariat capturing state power in itself provides no evidence of its emancipation from the communal, casteist, patriarchal value-system. As David Harvey (*Modernity and Its Future,* Stuart Hall (ed.) writes about the limitations of such conception which locates transformation predominantly in state power and private property and assumes that these are the institutions that quintessentially reproduce authoritarian values: "Foucault breaks with the notion that power [what we preferred to call authoritarianism] is ultimately located within the state and abjures us to conduct an ascending analysis of power starting, that is, from its infinitesimal mechanisms which each have their own history, their own trajectory, their own techniques and tactics and then see how these mechanisms of power have been and continue to be invested, colonised, utilised, involuted, transformed, displaced, extended, etc, by ever more general mechanisms and by forms of global domination Close scrutiny of the micro-politics of power relations in different localities, contexts and social situations leads him to conclude that there is an intimate relation between the system of knowledge [what we preferred to call value-system] which codify techniques and practices for the exercise of social control and domination withing particular localised contexts. The prison, the asylum, the hospital, the university, the school, the psychiatrist's office [we may add religion, family, caste] are all examples of sites where a dispersed and piecemeal organisation of power is built up independently of any systematic strategy of class domination." He further writes, "The only way open to climinte fascism in our heads is to explore and huild upon the open qualities of human discourse, and thereby intervene in the way knowledge is produced and constituted at the particular site where a localised power-discourse prevails." (Foucault's work, for instance, with prisoners was not aimed at producing reforms in state practices, but dedicated to the cultivation and enhancement of localised resistance to the institutions, techniques and discourses of organised repression.)

The thrust of this discourse has been that it is only through a multi-faceted and pluralist attack upon localised practices of repression that any global challenge to an authoritarian system like capitalism might be mounted without replicating all the multiple repressions of capitalism in a new form. Such ideas appeal to the various people's movements that have sprung into existence in the contemporary polity and only a critical analysis of their mode of functioning and a conviction in their potential to democratise the civil society can bring us out of the present chaos.

Published in the *Economic and Political Weekly*, March 30, 1996.

29

K. Balagopal: A Memory to be Lived

In one of my last conversations with Balagopal, in reply to my query about what it has been like building the Human Rights Forum (HRF), as they completed ten years, he replied that though the organisation had a presence in most of the districts of Andhra Pradesh, there was generally a decline of idealism. There was an unwillingness to launch and nurture struggles. In a more reflective mood, he later added, for movements to survive, we need some degree of innocence. It is this innocence that Balagopal seems to have well preserved with integrity, for himself. He had the rare courage of giving an issue all he had, yet make a starkly realist reading of what it is turning out to be.

The fact was that the degree of his own involvement with an issue or an organisation or a movement in no identifiable measure influenced his analysis. He combined a keen intellectual inquisitiveness, patient enough to bear with the open-endedness and the fluidity of ideas, and ideals that any theorist requires, with a single-mindedness of an activist. He combined a resolve to walk all the way in search of that distant goal, with an anxiety to achieve what is best possible in the here and now of politics; he seemed to have overcome that enduring gap in radical protest politics between following the trails of the unknown or yet-to-be-known with the unflinching commitment to one's own beliefs; he lived what he talked; he combined the distant public with the most intimate of personal; he seemed to have practised the insurmountable of contradictions with élan, an ease that almost made it invisible, that one would certainly miss unless one keenly followed the man himself.

Source of Inexhaustible Energy

What made Balagopal more than the civil rights activist that the world knows is a complexity that has to be caringly peeled out from the reams that he tucked in, within himself, so that he did not stand out, but looked as ordinary as is possible. His relentless pursuit of this ordinariness that did not come to him naturally revealed to the world as much perhaps as it also hid. I had once asked him, as if he had a key to the world tucked within: "Where do you get these inexhaustible energies from?" only to be greeted with a smile that is difficult to forget. A smile that warmly welcomed you to live it for yourself. This invite, seems to very briefly speak of a self that was intractably inverting the social logic as we know it.

He was, perhaps, attempting to combine a passion for details with an informed detachment; to contribute to a process without the self itself requisitioning anything from it. The effort itself carried the traces of the dispensability, and as much of a struggle not to become a site but amorphous enough so that our attention remained on the task next on hand. His anxiety was to formidably deal with power in all its forms without giving it the slightest opportunity to consolidate around himself. He seemed to have internalised this till it came naturally to him. He lived this in all its spatial and temporal dimensions. His attitude to suffering made it seem that it can be felt differently. His unwillingness to slow down was as much about his concern for the growing forms of violence, from state initiated to the more insidious ones, as it was about making sure of the absent self that seemed to be patiently waiting to make a comeback, just in case. Practice, in its most elementary sense for him meant this double-edged effort that can only but be tireless and incessant.

His mission of unsettling the darkest sides of power was invariably combined and carefully crafted with the most finest, intimate and affable of human selves. He once wrote, "to condemn oppression is to condemn at least a little bit of oneself".

Balagopal believed that "an exclusively critical attitude is useless as a guide for any transformative—as distinct from critical—activity excepting the seizure of power by force".

He was all alone in the forefront in naming police officers in Andhra Pradesh involved in extra-judicial violence and in demanding that murder charges be framed against them, in pointing to the hidden role of mafia, mercenaries appointed by the police, and their nexus with land mafia.

He wrote some of his masterpieces against Chandrababu Naidu and Y.S. Rajashekar Reddy, when they were riding high on power, before the dust had settled and the powers that be looked capable of unleashing the worst, with the added possibility of escaping under the cover of the din. The fear of the possibility of his death in the most unnoticed of fashions was something that gripped me on many occasions, as much due to the kind of "Constitutional State" that we have, as because of his very own resolved attitude towards death, almost matter of fact and nonchalant.

The best of his dark humour was pristinely kept for this. He once told us he had kept a scenic place over the Krishna river from where he would jump to death, if he were to contract a terminal disease (knowing well that his lifestyle would guarantee him nothing). His liberation from the tyranny that death can unleash on the living was part of his being, and complete. The script of his liberation was deeply aware of the momentariness and transient nature of the present as part of the long course of history that had the capacity to eerily equalise everything. His amiable willingness to stand alone when needed and be lost in the background was so easy in his world that it almost merited no attention. Being part of mass movements and leading an untiring public life, he seemed to have yet managed to enjoy the spaciousness of anonymity, impatient with adulations and dodging image traps, often amused at the self-propelling tendencies and instrumental attitudes that look legitimate since the ends we fought for were so ideal, so much a part of the organisational culture all around us. In being careful not to trespass into a space where others could grow, learn and think for themselves, he often withdrew in order to stand together rather than imagining himself standing for others. Critical engagement, he believed, was more dignifying than the consensus of patronage. In retrospect one feels, radical beliefs are as much a part of the collective social context we construct as is an individual effort that needs to set its own norms that it would unfailingly follow, independent of the consequences it invited. It seems to be imperative to internalise at least some norms and practice them for themselves, otherwise there seems to be no known way of translating the social and sustaining it at the level of the individual.

Mannerisms

Balagopal seemed to have believed that certain forms of solitariness went beyond the bourgeois notions of privacy, and without a self that was resolved with itself, its promise to be part of the long march of radical protest would more often than not end abruptly and inexplicably, leaving more despair and cynicism than it would be otherwise. In a society plagued by relations of patronage and dependence on leadership that is expansive enough to reduce the bulk of us into legitimately mute spectators his was a demeanour that was almost mistaken for being indifferent. There was a sense of brevity and minimality to the way he did things, the way he flung his arms around himself while making the most pungent of comments, and the way he delivered his public lectures, and we are told the way he argued his cases in the court. People often very strangely felt intimate and intimidated, elated and neglected in a single moment of friendship and togetherness with him was not constrained by mutuality and ties of obligation but enriched by compassion for those not known to you. A compassion that was not based on a contract but one that surrounded you to secure your dignity, that stayed with you, and within you. His abstruse mannerisms were a comment on the need to look for new ways of being.

The inverted and invisible world of Balagopal had everything to do, and was inextricably linked, to his politics and growing ethical concerns about those politics. It was not a practice that glorified sacrifice but it was indeed a sacrifice that glorified practice. A practice that believed that unless the complexities of structures are not reduced to simple and knowable values they not only fail to become part of the manifold experiences and lived practices, but create a distant public, only to reappear as opaque structures that wield insurmountable power.

Balagopal punctured the political with the personal and the intimate, and the latter with simplicity and modesty. He was known to leave appointments with ministers if they failed to keep their time and kept you waiting if he had to tend to his son. He would have plenty of jokes about himself, his compatriots, and especially, about those with a "cult status" in public life; he would have the keenest eye for detail when you expected it the least. In this mosaic, he championed new causes where the old did not suffice; sensed the need to protect what has been achieved (language of rights, rule of law, constitutions that promise social justice, among others), and fostered all that is fascinating and fragile including lifestyles, and culture.

I still vividly remember his trip to Kolkata when I had invited him to come and visit the university I was then working at. Soon after his talk, he left for a long walk for about four hours since he liked the leisurely conversations at public places in the city (as against his staunch dislike for Delhi, where he said he could not stay for more than a day since everything was loud and in-your-face!), it was quite something for someone who was himself impatient with long conversations. It is as important to cherish what is good here and now, as it is to struggle against that the ugly impoverishment all around us. Otherwise, strug- gles themselves could suffer the poverty of positive energy needed for rebuilding themselves. He believed that "this rebuilding has wrongly been seen as a direct continuation of the struggle against injustice. This notion that the force that is necessary to destroy unjust social structures will by itself lead to the reconstruction of society on a just basis… has been sufficiently proved an illusion by the happenings of this century".

Abrupt Life, Abrupt Departure

Balagopal, as in life, made his point in the way he left. His death was abrupt and his task seemed incomplete (if at all there can be anything complete for a life such as this). And the grief undoubtedly tough to overcome for a long time to come. But in grief I was not alone, nor was it restricted to the organisations and individuals he interacted with in the course of his activities, not even limited to the scores of groups and communities that got ameliorated through his tireless activism. It poignantly seemed to have engulfed all those who hardly knew and had only heard of him. It was intriguing to see friends who otherwise seemed to have not known him personally, complain of a loss that was inexplicable even to them. Individuals from various walks of life, who have written to Telugu dailies over the last week, shared the way their lives and world around them had come to a standstill. As Velcheru Narayan Rao wrote, "there seemed to be utter darkness in broad day light". Balagopal, so to say, had no constituency, though he had politics. This sense of loss seems to be as much for what he did as the way he did. His memory needs to be lived over and over. The world that was within him is now ours, and is the world we need to build. While radical politics will have to pause and look to intensely learn from the man, his life and his philosophy, scores of struggles need to move quickly in order to find ways of suspending all instrumental attitudes, sectarian claims and an undue privileging of ends over means, for he demonstrated that it is possible to do things differently.

Published in the *Economic and Political Weekly,* November 2009.

DALIT POLITICS AND RESERVATIONS

30

BSP: The Trap at the Centre

The birth anniversary of Babasaheb Ambedkar was marked by a slew of advertisements issued by BSP chief and Uttar Pradesh Chief Minister Mayawati in leading dailies. She also unveiled her own statue to mark the occasion. This renewed assertion of the BSP's ownership of Ambedkar's memory and legacy comes in the context of the BSP's broader efforts to shift its mobilisation strategy—not counting the short interlude when Mayawati seemed to go back to political square one as she took on Tikait recently—from one that targets the 'bahujan' to one that speaks to the 'sarvajan'.

Those loyal to the BSP believe that this shift was necessary to tame Brahminism. After all, it's for the first time that upper caste leaders are getting elected from and serving a party that essentially belongs to the Dalits and OBCs. Apart from enabling the BSP to wrest political power, this also helps in infusing confidence among Dalits. However, those Dalit scholars who think and work within a moral idiom and the more idealistic among Dalit youth feel shortchanged. They see this shift to sarvajan mobilisation as a form of political opportunism, if not a wholesale moral degeneration.

According to this argument, the BSP's new strategy not only robs Dalits of their right to assert and protest but also betrays the fundamentals of Ambedkarite philosophy that emphasise reclaiming the community's dignity above everything else. In this paradigm, the achieving or sharing of political power was but one possible means, though an important one, of pursuing this large social and philosophical vision.

But the shift to the centrism that the sarvajan philosophy

represents, while being new to the way the Dalit empowerment agenda has been pursued in the post-Independence period, has been integral to the way parliamentary democracy has evolved and survived in India. There is a sense of inevitability and even indispensability to the way a centrist framework needs to be worked out and followed to remain close to the portals of power, especially at the Centre.

The Congress Party inherited the Gandhian legacy of the 'politics of accommodation', the art of putting together contradictory and oppositional political and social forces and principles. The 'Congress System' or the 'umbrella party' built itself on the basis of the philosophy of Gandhian trusteeship, by managing industrialists and rich farmers on the one hand and the landless on the other. It came to proudly claim the trust of all castes, classes and regions.

In 1989, the resurgence of the BJP was marked by an aggressive sectoral mobilisation of upper caste Hindus against the Muslims around the demand of a Ram temple at Ayodhya. Yet when the BJP managed to cobble together a ruling alliance called the NDA, it had to not only keep in abeyance the core of its Hindu nationalist agenda, including the abolition of Article 370, implementation of the uniform civil code, and building of the Ram temple, but it also had to be seen to distance itself from the more brazen members of the Sangh Parivar including the Vishwa Hindu Parishad and Bajrang Dal. The requirement of a larger share of seats made it imperative for the BJP to spread in the south and therefore it dropped its insistence on Hindi as the national language. For similar reasons, the BJP is constrained to express jubilation over the recent Supreme Court verdict on the implementation of reservations for OBCs in institutions of higher education. This centrist churning continues to haunt the BJP in its renewed bid to come to power in the next general elections. The party must strike a balance between the gains from moving to the Centre and the losses it incurs by compromising on its ideological purity.

In this backdrop, the shift from bahujan to sarvajan is the BSP's way of moving towards the Centre. Mayawati has grasped the significance of moving beyond exclusivist mobilisation. While such a strategy might bring a party to power it will not sustain it in power for long. In a polarised state like UP, Mayawati's strategy to extend the BSP vote share by drawing in the upper castes has not only changed its image but may have made it a serious contender at the Centre.

Undoubtedly, this shift has weakened the single-mindedness of its campaign against atrocities on Dalits and has blunted its aggressive mobilisation for recognition and redistribution of resources for the Dalits. By this reckoning, the BSP is losing its ideological purity like the BJP and attempting to emerge as an umbrella party like the Congress. While centrism allows you a new social base it also makes your traditional social base very shaky. Centrist parties simply have no language to keep any particular social base tightly with them. Thus, while the Brahmin vote bank can shift to the BSP, the Dalit vote bank could as well shift to the Congress.

It is in this context that Mayawati is jittery about Rahul Gandhi's appeal to Dalit youth in particular and Dalits in general. In essence, the appeal of Dalit rhetoric without substantive ground-level empowerment is not very different from the appeal of dynasty. More than anyone else, Mayawati understands this well.

Published in *The Indian Express*, April 17, 2008.

31

Dalits, Parliament, and 'Politics of Presence'

Review of Rise of the Plebians? The Changing Face of the Indian Legislative Assemblies *edited by Christopher Jaffrelot (Routledge, Delhi, 2010).*

The book under review is a quantitative demonstration of the growing 'politics of presence' as a nodal point of democratisation with the underlying presumption, as Anne Phillips observed, 'that changing the composition of decision-making bodies changes the character of the issues and policies discussed'. It, however, pursues this mode of argument with a singular focus on caste as the key variable when compared especially with class, and therefore the editors of the volume believe that the main objective of the book 'is to study how India's caste-based social diversity translated into politics in a dynamic perspective, over more than 60 years, at the state level'.'Politics of presence', however, has played itself in the theatre of Indian politics constrained by its close cousin, 'politics of accommodation', better known as centrism as the Rudolphs have termed it. It is the imperative of centrist politics that also explains the centrality of caste as against class politics. It is, in a sense, unique to Indian social formation and the more operative part of the Indian politics that democracy has evolved more through 'adjustment rather than displacement'. True to the ethos of liberal democracy, the process of democratisation and its limits in India while has been slow and incremental on the one hand, has also been stable and functional on the other. This combinatory posturing of a certain kind of passivity with stability and change, also referred to as 'passive revolution', is possible precisely due to the overwhelmingly centrist nature of Indian polity. Centrism, while allowing for change, also regulates and disciplines it, and in the process opens avenues for varied and often contradictory permutations and combination of alliances between differently located social forces. The saga of the 'Rise of the Plebeians' in India is marred by this uneven and at times a very serendipitous process, which is what has been attempted to be captured by this book through a plethora of empirical data and statistics regarding the social (read caste) composition of the representatives to the legislative assemblies of states from various regions.

These include the Hindi belt with focus on Uttar Pradesh, Madhya Pradesh and Bihar; Punjab, Rajasthan and Gujarat within the northwestern region; the Deccan plateau including Maharashtra, Karnataka and Andhra Pradesh; areas populated by the Adivasis such as Jharkhand and Chhattisgarh; both the states that have been dominated by Communist rule—West Bengal and Kerala; states that have been the 'domain of proportionality' including Delhi and Himachal Pradesh; and finally, the case of Tamil Nadu as representative of the 'subalternist tradition'. Chapters focusing on each of these states trace a veritable trajectory of the history of caste dynamics in legislative assemblies primarily bringing into relief the interface between the so-called upper castes, OBCs and the Dalits, essentially mapping the shift from the predominance of the so-called upper castes to the newlyemerging dominance of the OBCs and Dalits and the ever-changing alliances between all of them. We could, perhaps, argue that centrism itself has three variations in the context of Indian politics. It has a political dimension where it manifests itself through moderation of political ideologies and alliances between contradictory and even conflicting social forces.

It has an economic dimension wherein the rise of intermediary classes and caste groups—to allude again to what the Rudolphs have referred to as the 'Bullock Capitalists'—marks not only a class balance but also one between industry and agriculture or rural and urban. Such economic dynamics in turn have political ramifications in terms of political alliances and party programmes.

Finally, the cultural variation of centrism could get expressed through an overarching commonality of cultural markers that either disallows caste specific political variation or even if it does, the subaltern 'speaks' the same language. Hindi belt is, perhaps, the best representative case for political centrism. As Jaffrelot remarks, in his Introduction, 'in all these states, the proportion of the upper-caste MLAs has steadily declined from about 40–55% in the 1950s to about 25–35% today whereas the share of the OBC grew from 10–20% to about 20–40%'. Similar is the story of meteoric rise in the representation for the Dalits with the rise of the Bahujan Samaj Party (BSP). However, while in 1993 there were no upper-caste MLAs in the BSP, by 1998 15% of the party's MLAs were from the so-called upper castes including Brahmins. Intriguingly, as the chapter on UP notes 'the rise in the upper-caste MLAs had been achieved at the expense of SCs whose share in the party's representation in the Assembly had gone down to 30%'. This in turn had an impact on the part y's ideological programme including the more recent shift to the rhetoric of 'sarvajan' replacing its earlier anti-Brahmin alliance of the 'bahujan'. Political centrism of this kind seems to entail the growth of the phenomenon of 'coalition of extremes', including the obverse side the active participation of a section of Dalits in the state-sponsored pogrom in Gujarat, which in future might have a distinct manifestation through a changing social composition of the MLAs of BJP. The Deccan Plateau in general seems to be representative of centrism that draws its centripetal forces primarily through the economic processes. This region has witnessed 'unchallenged rule of dominant castes' that are quintessentially peasant proprietary or the rich farmer class. They have been instrumental in supporting the creation of regional parties, such as the Telugu Desam Party (TDP) in Andhra Pradesh, to create new avenues to invest the surplus generated from agriculture,into emerging sectors such as the film, hotel and construction industries, as against the industries already supported by the centre. It was this context that enabled the TDP to forge an alliance between the upwardly mobile backward castes (40–50% of the state's population) and the dominant kamma caste, articulating what was famously referred to as 'Bharat vs. India' by Sharad Joshi.

Finally, West Bengal is the best representative case for what could be referred to as cultural centrism. Although land reforms has benefited Dalits and other backward castes, it has strangely resulted in the process of 'invisibilisation of caste' in the public sphere since what is recognised is class which has ironic convergence with the rule of dominant castes and elite bhadralok culture. As the chapter on West Bengal questions, 'are bhadraloks, then, still in power in today's West Bengal? These "respectable people", an urban elite enjoying the multiple privileges of upper-caste status, English education and employment in the higher professions has been dominating the public life of Bengal since the 1930s'. The dominant bhadralok culture continues to create conditions for the Dalits and backward castes to depend on the patronage of the party.

This framework although not explicitly stated in the book could be helpful in approaching the issues, which is otherwise quantitatively dense and rather thin in terms of the theoretical framework, and the conceptual categories that writers deploy in their analysis. It is unfortunate that it does not help much in overcoming the rather enduring wedge between quantitative/empirical and qualitative/theoretical divide in social sciences in general. It, however, creates the possibilities of raising various conceptual issues in understanding the nature of democratisation through representative democracy. The chapter on Delhi raises, for instance, the interesting issue of a Dalit getting elected from a non-reserved constituency, which perhaps is the direction that 'politics of presence' should eventually take to bridge the yawning gap between representation and participation. The various narratives of the quick-fix and yet very tenuous alliances suggests the shift to what David Held refers to as 'strategic legitimacy' where not just the weak but even the dominant castes operate as vote-banks. The detailed chronicles of the changing influence of various caste groups also provide an occasion to think of the interface between the high politics in the electoral domain and the non-party political movements in states such as Tamil Nadu and other states with strong Dalit movements. Apart from being useful in guiding us to much wanted data on the changes that have taken place in terms of caste equations within political parties and their representatives in the legislative assemblies, it will also be a very helpful read in explaining the backdrop of the current changes such as the success of Trinamool Congress in West Bengal and failure of Praja Rajyam Party in Andhra Pradesh. In the end, one cannot miss appreciating the arduous efforts made by both the editors and the individual contributors in diligently bringing together a mass of absolutely crucial quantitative data from the 1950s onwards and no doubt it has taken them more than 10 years in putting it all together . Apart from academics and researches, in the end this should be a must-read for all students to have a concrete sense of the abstract concepts they are introduced to at the postgraduate level.

Published in the *Journal of South Asian History and Culture*,
Vol. 1, Issue 1, 2009.

32

Dalits, OBCs and Stigma

The caste system has become a permanent feature of the social, political, and material dimensions of Indian reality. The effects of the caste system permeate not merely the dynamics of redistribution, but also recognition and representation. While, certain measures have been implemented to mitigate the ill and adverse impacts of the system on the processes of redistribution, the impacts on the issues of recognition and representation remain both understudied and neglected. One of the critical dimensions of a caste-ridden psyche is the generation of self-contempt amongst those suffering under the caste-hierarchy. The caste system reproduces itself when the victims themselves believe that he or she is not worthy of respect. This belief is made possible through various rituals and philosophical propositions, such as the Karma theory, that are converted into common sense and through other related performative dimensions of the caste system. Dr. B.R. Ambedkar, who has been the leading proponent of the struggles against caste-based discrimination and was the architect of the Indian Constitution, was one of the few Dalit (i.e. former untouchables) leaders who realised the importance and the inter-connection between all three dimensions-redistribution, recognition and representation. In fact, it was around the issue of how much/how to combine the material with the cultural or psychological that Ambedkar and Gandhi strongly differed. Gandhian strategy almost replaced the issue of the material with the moral, while Ambedkar was attempting to combine the two and look for modes where one did not negate the other. He, therefore, argued for strong state-intervention and the implementation of welfare measures to achieve material amelioration. He suggested the policy of reservations, or affirmative action, in jobs (economic), education (social) and parliament (political). Ambedkar was conscious that anti-caste struggles were not merely about achieving a few jobs, the struggle was to regain 'dignity,' 'honour ,' and 'title deeds' (property). While on one hand, he wanted to use the power of caste as a community, on the other, he propounded large-scale conversion of Dalits to move outside the fold of Hinduism.

Reservations Against Recognition: Deeply Conflicted

The system of reservations refers to a policy framework that allows for jobs and seats in government-run institutions to be reserved—as quotas—in proportion to the population of the so-called lower castes, including the scheduled castes and scheduled tribes. It was decided at the time of the Constitution-making process that 23 per cent would be reserved for the so-called lower caste groups. India has, since then, been following this provision and implementing what has come to be referred to as reservations. The wide-scale belief was that such a policy would provide new opportunities for the disadvantaged social groups, and produce, in due course, elites who can effectively represent the interests of the Dalits. However, the policies of affirmative action or reservations seem to create an inherent conflict between the processes of redistribution and the demands for recognition. While it is a fact that the policies of reservation have created new opportunities for the specific disadvantaged social groups, these however have come at a cost of causing the intangible injury of mis-recognition. 'The result is to mark the most disadvantaged class as inherently deficient and insatiable, as always needing more and more. In time, such a class can come to appear privileged, the receipt of special treatment and underserved largesse.

Thus, an approach aimed at redressing injustices of distribution can end up creating injustices of recognition.

A Troubled Elite Leadership

Moreover, the elites produced out of the system of reservations themselves remained stigmatised seen to be less meritorious and enjoying undue benefits at the cost of the nation's resources. In spite of various struggles and new mobilisation strategies, Dalits in India continue to be stigmatised and continue to face new forms of discrimination in the modern public sphere, institutions of higher learning, the market, and civil society. For instance, when Dalits join institutions of higher learning such as a university like Jawaharlal Nehru University in Delhi, they continue to be socially discriminated in terms of the patterns of socialisation, they face difficulties with English as a medium of education and teaching, among many other problems. These limitations further reinforce their sense of stigma. The question that is pertinent for democracy in India to have substantive meaning is: how can Dalits overcome stigma and attain a civic status that allows them to enjoy liberty, equality, and fraternity?

Constitutional Protection for 'Backward Classes': The Second Democratic Surge

Signposts to such an emancipation could well lie in the new sociological and political changes that India is currently witnessing. Perhaps what the Dalit struggles since independence could not achieve could well be possible with these changes. The foremost amongst these is the new wave of reservations that India has adopted since the 1990s. The Constitution of India, along with reservations to the Dalits also provides scope to reserve opportunities to 'backward classes.' The Constitution, under Article 340, provided provision for a commission to look into the issue of 'backward classes.' Until the First Backward Classes Commission was set up in 1953, there was no definite meaning or method of identifying which social groups constituted these classes and what role caste had in it. The Janata Government in 1977 set up the Mandal Commission, which argued that class in many senses in India approximates caste; therefore it identified 3743 caste groups as 'Other Backward Classes' (OBCs), comprising 52 per cent of the total population. However, the Mandal Commission report faced resistance and the Janata Government failed to implement its recommendations as it lost power to the Congress by the time the report was submitted. It was only in 1990 that the V.P. Singh government took up the recommendations and announced its implementation. This new wave of reservations—also referred to as the 'second democratic upsurge'—I believe, is set to change the stigma attached to the discourse of reservations in India. This may be possible, first due to the reservations to the OBCs, part of which are politically and economically powerful. For the first time in India, an already existing elite section of the population would be part of the 'reserved category.'

What Do Dalits Want?

Demands from dominant groups (caste groups such as Jats and Rajputs) are gradually making reservations a more generalised feature of the Indian polity, rather than being identified with any specific caste, community, or class. This, in turn, makes it very difficult for the so-called forward or upper castes to denounce or stigmatise the discourse of reservations. Instead, this debate has headed in the direction of 'reverse social osmosis' by seeking reservation for the poor among the upper castes. There is now a proposal in India to provide 5 per cent reservations for the poor among the Brahmins. A proposal for 33 per cent reservations for women in Parliament is pending, and it is expected that the Parliament will pass it soon. Various proposals to reserve opportunities for Muslims, based on the findings of the Sachar Committee, for disabled individuals and other disadvantaged sections of the society are the focus of the recently set up Equal Opportunities Commission.

Quotas: A Time Sensitive Issue

A second reason why the stigma attached to reservations may be weakening is that the reservation policy for OBCs has introduced the new 'creamy layer' criterion. This means that those above a certain income (in this case Rs 4.5 lakh per annum) are not eligible to get reservations. This not only removes elites and well-to-do sections from getting the benefits of reservations but it also introduces the idea that eservations are a time-bound mechanism and not a permanent policy. Even Ambedkar argued that the reservations for the scheduled castes and scheduled tribes needed to be restricted to a period of ten years, although he had restricted this criterion to the case of reservations in political representation. We need to revisit this issue to see if the time-bound criterion can be applied to the reservations for Dalits in jobs and higher education. Time-bound reservations seem to be necessary to achieve both redistribution and recognition.

Affirmative Action: Will It Be Successful?

Finally, OBCs approach the idea of merit very differently. The Dalits, for various reasons, dichotomised reservations and merit into two watertight compartments. Most argued that the very idea of merit was bogus—a fraudulent construct of the upper castes. However, they did not provide an alternative basis for the working of public institutions. So in the process, Dalits remained permanent 'outsiders' to the public institutions. The question remained unanswered as to whether institutions can play their role and whether reservations alone would serve their purpose merely by giving proportional representation to individuals who belong to the so-called lower caste. However, the OBCs seem to be combining reservations, competition, efficiency, and merit in new ways that are not mutually exclusive. Those who lack opportunities can also be meritorious if given the chance. Is it not important that there are further mechanisms, such as teaching extra courses of English, so that everyone can perform well within the system? This newfound confidence can go a long way in refuting the attempts to stigmatise certain social groups as inherently and innately 'backward.'

Published in the *Canada Watch*, 2011.

33

Everyday Life of Reservations

India has one of the most extensive protective discrimination policy frames in the world. The policy of reservations has greatly contributed in providing job and educational opportunities to some of the most deprived and socially marginalised castes.

Yet, rather surprisingly, there is very little debate on reservations in institutions of higher learning. It begs three important questions: What type of prejudices does it create? What type of institutional dilemmas does it lead to? What are the changes that are necessary to allow those who get into institutions of higher learning, both as students and faculty, to realise their highest potential?

Individuals entering institutions have had to carry the cross of prejudice on their backs ever since the policy was introduced. Some of the forms it has taken have been to often leave the reserved posts vacant, declare that they have not found suitable candidates, even as recruitment to the open/general posts has often been severely compromised on in terms of merit. It has never been the case that interview boards ever failed to find a suitable candidate for the open posts. Similarly, there is tremendous resistance in appointing candidates from SC, ST and OBC backgrounds to the open posts; if they are found to be meritorious then they are generously accommodated within their respective quotas.

With regard to admission of students, wherever there is provision for viva, then it is seen to that students fill in their respective quotas. The caste of the student, wherever information is not available, is gathered through the surname, body language, colour of the skin, dress sense, rural-urban differentiation, and proficiency in English. It is this underlying bias that has led the students union in Jawaharlal Nehru University to demand the reduction of viva voce marks from its current 30 marks to 15. It has been found in a recent RTI filed by the students' union that there is a clear discrepancy between written and viva marks in various centres. Similar has been the case with other apex bodies such as the UPSC.

Prejudice is not the only stumbling block; there are genuine institutional dilemmas that a policy of reservation creates. For instance, once the candidates from these backgrounds enter institutions of higher learning, then there are no protective measures available and are assessed by the general standards. Often it is a dilemma as to how we evaluate the performance of such students. It is found that students might not cross the minimum threshold. This either leads to ad-hocism in somehow pushing through the students or it results in high dropout rates and difficulties in coping with the academic rigours. There is an impending need to devise new methods of evaluation. For instance, each student could be evaluated from her or his own background performance. If they have scored a certain percentage at undergraduate level, then it can be progressively compared with their current performance. The difference could be the mark of their performance rather than an absolute standard that current system of evaluation imposes on them. This can institutionalise a method of accounting for diversity and difference, while maintaining uniformity and standardisation (and might also actually offer us an opportunity to realise "unity in diversity").

Finally, institutional and systemic changes are necessary to allow faculty and students to realise their highest potential, which is what drives the philosophy behind the policy of reservations, and not merely provide representation in proportion to their percentage in population. We need to assess the specific challenges they face that could include remedial courses in teaching English, debate on the nature of the syllabus, cultural difficulties faced in transition from rural to urban settings, access to library facilities, among other such factors.

With regard to the recruitment of faculty members, recently the government has approved of reservations in promotion and recruitment at higher posts rather than merely to entry level posts. While this is a welcome move, this should however be accompanied by certain qualifications, such as publications, and teaching experience for those wishing to be promoted through reserved posts. What kind of minimum qualifying markers ought to be put in place need to be seriously debated, including if the same method of "background performance" kind of evaluation mode can be used for members of the faculty too. Unfortunately, these have either not been the concern of those championing reservations or they have summarily resisted these changes out of fear of prejudice. It should be now important to realise that a sense of achievement is imperative for both allowing the realisation of their highest potential and to avoid empowerment translating into patronage.

The vocal voices among the dalits and the OBCs need to move beyond merely looking for prejudice in the system at the level of intention, and appreciate the genuine institutional dilemmas that a policy of reservations creates. Without this, dalits and OBCs might gain entry into institutions of higher learning but fail to identify and appropriate them, as much as enable themselves in realising their highest potential.

Published in the Sunday Magazine, *The Hindu*, May 26, 2013.

34

Reservations: Caste versus Economic Criterion

One debate that does not take a backseat even in a busy electoral season is that of reservations. Recently, Congress leader Rahul Gandhi evinced interest in introducing affirmative action in the private sector, which is a move away from caste-based quota-system that we have followed for educational and job opportunities for the Dalits and the Other Backward Classes (OBCs).

It has often been the argument of the upper castes that they would support a system of reservations if it were to be on economic grounds, instead of caste. They further believe that caste-based reservations only help the well-off sections within the castes getting the benefit of reservations, leaving out the most deserving sub-groups and individuals. What is the real merit of this argument?

Constitution makers of India did recognise the validity of this argument, given that India was one of the poorest countries in world when it gained its Independence. The Constitution under Article 340 did provide a provision to set up a panel to look into the issue of 'backward classes.' It very consciously uses the language of classes and not caste.

However, there was no definite meaning or method of identifying which social groups constituted these classes. The first backward classes panel or the Kaka Kalelkar Commission set up in 1953, gave its report in 1955, recommending special benefits to various caste groups that operated like classes in the Indian context. It must, however, be noted that Kalelkar himself refuted the recommendations of the Commission he headed arguing instead that caste-based reservations were "repugnant to the spirit of democracy since in democracy it is the individual, not the family or the caste, which is the unit."

He instead recommended that all individuals whose family income was less than Rs 800 annually need to get special economic and educational aid from the government.

The point, however, was whether individuals were marginalised due to pure economic logic or was the economic status itself determined by other social and cultural factors of belonging to specific communities, or more specifically, caste groups. In other words, if individuals, belonging to all caste groups, had evenly remained backward then individual or family as the unit would have made sense but if individuals had been marginalised due to their caste position in society, wouldn't it make sense to remove that caste-based impediment? It is for this reason that individuals belonging to certain castes remained backward in comparison with those from other well-to-do caste groups.

It was based on this reasoning that the Kaka Kalelkar Commission identified a list of 2,399 backward groups on the basis of the various criteria including place in trade and occupation, security of employment, educational attainment, representation in government service, and position in the social hierarchy.

This was followed up when the Janata Party government in 1977 set up the next panel—Mandal Commission—to again look into the feasibility of providing reservations to deserving backward classes/castes. The Commission again emphasised the role of caste in structuring opportunities and backwardness. Though it applied 11 different indicators to identify backward groups, they overlapped with specific caste groups. Finally, the Commission identified 3,743 caste groups as OBCs comprising 52 per cent of the total population.

Quota and RTE

However, the role of special provisions on economic criterion does not end with backward classes commissions. More recently, the central government under the Right to Education Act reserved 25 per cent of the seats for children from economically and socially weaker sections in public and also private/corporate schools.

What then has been the response of the more privileged upper castes to this provision based 'purely' on income? Many of the private and corporate schools have resisted implementation of this provision, again in the name of diluting standards, while the parents of children from privileged upper caste backgrounds continue to lament the prospect of their children studying alongside the wards of their maids and drivers. They instead prefer more homogenised and sanitised schooling system that is equivalent with their social status and everyday life in gated communities and 'enclaves.'

This move to break this homogeneity is being perceived as undoing the economic and social mobility, represented by the capacity to segregate themselves with the rest of the population groups—that they have attained over a few generations. Upper castes that have all along argued for reservations on 'pure' economic basis now stand as disapproving of RTE as they were of caste-based reservations.

However, the same castes that wax eloquent about merit have little compunction in paying capitation fees in private institutions, which should have been ideally perceived as a 'murder of merit.' Similarly, social capital and networking play a significant role in the opportunities that these caste groups land up with and have very little to do either with the merit or proficiency for the jobs they are selected for.

The way forward from here is really a judicious expansion of the net of reservations for religious minorities, women and even the poor among the Brahmins. This expansion, however, needs to be combined with greater investment in public education that should ideally move towards the Common Neighbourhood Schooling system, where all children, irrespective of their socio-economic background, study in these schools.

Children of all castes, classes and religious backgrounds need to do their schooling together, simply to understand the nature of diversity and differences in the world. It is through this system that the United States today has the highest inter-generational mobility. For this, the public discourse in India needs to move towards accepting an inclusive social system on caste and economic grounds, overcome social prejudices and above all give up the search to emerge as elites through social separation.

Published in the *Deccan Herald,* May 5, 2014.

35

Caste and Civil Society

Review of Civility Against Caste: Dalit Politics and Citizenship in Western India *by Suryakant Waghmore (Sage, Delhi, 2014).*

This book once again foregrounds the ongoing debate on how to approach and conceptualise civil society in India. Is civil society a 'realm of freedom' or a realm of hegemony? Is it a 'bourgeois society' that introduces the processes of individuation and breakdown of community relations or enables in forging civic ethos and civic community as against traditional hierarchies? The variations in approaching the concept of civil society are doubly compounded when we begin to discuss it in the context of caste. Part of the problem really seems to be while discourses and analysis, over the last few decades in India, has surged ahead exploring the various modes of democratisation, including ideas of 'secularisation of caste' and 'politicisation of caste', these have remained as very selective instances in the life and dynamics of caste based exclusion in India, and they highlight very marginal and partial achievements by the anti-caste movements. Caste-based practices continue to be predominantly violent, invoking everyday forms of exclusion and humiliation. For Suryakant Waghmore this reality does not get represented in the debates on how to approach civil society. It is in this, he argues that constitution of civility, and civil/civic spaces squarely belongs and is part of the emancipatory project of anti-caste movements. Anti-caste movements struggle routinely to construct these spaces and in the process are effectively attempting to construct and strengthen civil society in India. He says, 'the moral impediment that liberals favour of deliberative procedures, politeness, rational communication and undoing of status privileges in the practice of civil society are not antithetical to the freedom of Dalits. The liberal procedures and institutions of civil society are crucial to unsettle the traditional modes of civility that constructs dalits as lesser subjects' (p.202). Having said this, Waghmore does note the problem that the dalit movement itself deploys extra-institutional forms of mobilisation, including use of violent modes, which 'do not fit the liberal ethos'. Though he does not further interrogate this problematique, as to what is the concrete effect of this denial in the way dalit struggles are perceived, by those inhabiting and those aspiring to become new entrants of the civil society? Where is the faultline between the civil society as it exists and civil society as a aspirational ideal of those currently marginalised? How does the latter, in substantive sense, differ from the former idea of civil society? That domain which deploys and carries a range of practices that are declared to be uncivil in order to gain entrance to existing civil society, how does it transform it? Will it continue remain within the limits of liberal ethos or does it go beyond? Would it then be a category mistake to refer to this domain as essentially a liberal civil society that dalit struggles are constructing in course of their everyday interactions? These are some of the questions that can be posed in order to contextualise this book.

However, one can very much understand the core concern of Waghmore as someone responding to the insidious modes in which caste operates and excludes, based on his rather thick ethonography. It is therefore possible to understand his concern of moving from traditional hierarchies to contractual relations, in the liberal mode. Contractual relations offer basic protection, freedom as exchange relations, and secular options of exit. However, the same contractual relations thereby because they are based on contractual relations and quid pro quo relations, undermine ideals of solidarity and fraternity, instead promote instrumental reasoning. Again, how do we move beyond this impasse in the context of caste in India? This book provides us an opportunity to bring this issue into relief. Waghmore is also upfront in his critique of post-colonial scholars in their dismissal of civil society only as a domain of the elites, thereby *impso facto* 'condemning' the subaltern to an existence of incivility. Some of these theories neglect and undermine the subaltern aspiration to move into the realms of civility and civil society. However, even here we need to raise the issue that we alluded to before, how else do we then dignify the extra-institutional modes of mobilisation that Dalit movement itself resorts to, and which are consistently undermined by the liberal ethos? As Waghmore himself observes, in discussing the strategies of the BSP, that it has attempted 'substantialisation process of caste and not its annihilation', which is an acknowledgement of the postcolonial mode in anti-caste struggles. The shift to using caste itself in order to fight caste precisely moves beyond the known liberal mores, and this would be in contradiction with the basic thrust of what Suryakant argues. This, however, does not answer the question that the flip side of theorising this way by the postcolonial/subaltern scholarship undermines above all the aspirations of the subaltern themselves to move beyond their existing uncivil modes of existence, and in merely dignifying them, postcolonial scholarship becomes susceptible to reinstating oriental views of the subaltern in India. They also end up in a strange ways reinforcing the way subaltern is approached by the liberal ethos, exposing the moment where liberal ethos and the postcolonial ethos belong to the same 'epistemic community'. Part of the complexity is in the embedded multilayered character of caste itself. The best way could be to look for complex combinatory frames that can amalgamate these diverse yet interlinked dimensions of caste and civil society. Mere reinstating of a liberal frame while remains an important part of this reality, it is but only one of the dimensions. This book, in a sense, does not affirm this, and argues instead for the liberal, contractual relations as having the capacity to capture the essential dynamics internal to the anti-caste movement.

What is the possible way out of this impasse is a way too complex issue to be discussed here, though suffice it to say that scholarship on caste needs to raise a range of new questions, in relation to the old. How the insidious and violent forms of exclusions of Dalits has resulted in various strategies being combined together, and in that the Dalit movement has remained one of the most creative social forces. Along with this, the new scholarship also needs to open up the impact of this sustained violence on the political subjectivity of Dalits, in articulating sub-caste conflicts within dalits. The move in the Dalit politics from the 'Dalit panther' phase to the current phase of demanding institution of 'Dalit capitalism', moving from the project of forging 'Bahujan Samaj' beyond the singularity of dalit to growing conflicts between Dalits and the OBCs, and finally the success of the right-wing politics in mobilising and giving a new subjectivity to dalithood. These are further issues that are linked to those issues that we raised initially in terms of the liberal and postcolonial frames. In fact, the former modes of approaching caste might have something to do with this new visible shift in Dalit politics.

Published in the *Book Review*.

36

Dalits versus Muslims: The New Intra-Subaltern Conflict

How do you view the spurt of incidents of anti-Muslim violence across the country including persistence of communal tension in western UP?

India had a long tradition of communal violence but the recent incidents of anti-Muslim attacks in UP are a unique phenomenon. The uniqueness lies in the nature of conflicts, which are of low intensity with persistence of communal tensions, mostly fought between Dalits and Muslims and OBCs and Muslims. This is happening because the RSS and the BJP are gradually succeeding in saffronising Dalits and OBCs. Today a large chunk of subalterns are in the fold of the RSS and the BJP, which chased in on internal contradictions among lower castes. As a large section of lower castes are also oppressed by their dominant sub-castes, who are perceived to have cornered most of the opportunities in jobs, resources and politics, the most marginalised sections of Dalits and OBCS view the RSS and the BJP as providing an opportunity for social mobility. This aspect of lower caste politics was not understood by any parties other than the Hindu right. I have recently been in Telangana on fieldwork where I have noticed that OBCs in a large chunk are shifting to the BJP, which, in turn, supported the Telangana Movement. If this trend continues, the whole sections of OBCs will shift to the BJP in coming 10 years all across the country. Such trends are very dangerous as witnessed in Muzaffarnagar where OBCs have overwhelmingly supported the BJP.

How have the RSS and the BJP succeeded in saffronising Dalits and OBCs, who are the real victims of the Hindu social order?

Over the decades Indian politics has witnessed a gradual rightward shift of the lower castes. Why has this happened? I will offer a sociological explanation of this, which I call the phenomenon of entrenched caste psyche. While the fact remains that the caste, like a ladderlike structure, maintains a system of graded-inequality as every group has a dual-positionality with an oppressor above and the oppressed below, the anti-caste movements of India have exclusively addressed the dominance of the upper castes but never as much simultaneously articulated the caste hegemony towards those below by the very same sub-group/sub-caste. This intra-group domination has not been on the agenda of anti-caste movements. Instead, these movements are operating with big categories like Brahmins and non-Brahmins, upper caste, OBCs, Dalits, etc. What I want to underscore is that the caste psyche, to dominate those below you, remains unquestioned by anti-caste movements. This very caste psyche has pitted Dalits and OBCs against Muslims, whom I consider as the most vulnerable sections and universal target of society. Unfortunately, Left and progressive sections have remained oblivious of this dimension as they, instead of engaging with subaltern politics critically, have celebrated everything about them. The so-much celebrated Subaltern Studies, for example, have patronised the marginalised sections.

What do you have to say about the progressive aspect of lower caste assertion? Are you not undermining this?

I have never said that there is no progressive aspect of lower caste politics. I do consider its assertion as a part of process of democratisation. But there is also a failure of anti-caste movements. Long ago Ambedkar underscored an urgent need for annihilation of caste but that agenda has been now dismissed as a utopia. The next phase was secularisation of caste, whose apologists strongly argued that the lower castes' assertion is a secular upsurge as marginalised castes across religions became united in their struggle for social justice. But after its initial success, it soon gushed out as the RSS and the BJP were able to Hindutvaise the Bahujan sections. As I mentioned earlier the success of the RSS and the BJP lies in the unwillingness to anti-caste movements to raise the issue of intra-group domination. Who are the beneficiaries of reservations? Who are dominating lower caste politics? For example, OBC politics is dominated by one of two castes such as Yadavas and Kurmis in Bihar and Dalit politics by Malas in Andhra Pradesh, Mahars in Maharashtra and Chamars in UP. The other sub-castes among Dalits and OBCs are yet to be empowered. The intra-caste contradiction must be understood against this background. The OBC and Bahujan politics have not addressed this concern as it does not matter electorally. Do you think lower caste politics is serious about taking up the issue of snake charmer? Having perceived the possibility of an upward mobility through lower caste politics, the marginalised lot of lower castes is joining the RSS and the BJP. This gives them a sense of empowerment as they are now part of the majority. Their attraction towards the RSS and the BJP is also because of the fact that the dominant sections of lower caste politics such as Dalits in Andhra Pradesh, Maharashtra, Uttar Pradesh have converted to Christianity, Buddhism and Islam. They, therefore, are taking a route to Hinduism. The RSS and the BJP, in turn, have welcomed them and projected them as warriors of Hinduism so they are launching attacks on Muslims to prove their Hindu-ness.

What do you think about the nature of recent communal violence in western UP?

The BJP is operating with two strategies. I call it high intensity growth with low intensity communalism. Let me explain this. As Modi's Government at the Centre follows the Gujarat model of neoliberal economic policy with a view to achieving high growth, it cannot afford to go for high intensity episodic communal riots of the past. The BJP has realised that there is little acceptance for carnages like the Gujarat violence in 2002 among investors and middle classes. Moreover, the talk of governance by Modi does not sit well with big communal riots of the past. That is why the RSS and the BJP are not engineering a high intensity communal violence. Rather they are content with the insidious elimination of Muslims. This everyday elimination of Muslims is done by depriving them of their economic opportunity and rendering them politically insignificant. Even Congress is in a dilemma to give tickets to

Muslims as it does not want to appear pro-Muslim and thus anti-Hindu. One can see how much communal consciousness has penetrated at the bottom of our society that when I asked a Dalit in Punjab if caste mattered to him in poll, his answer was that he would vote a "meritorious" candidate. But when I asked him if he would vote for a Muslim candidate, his prompt reply was that Muslim *hamara aadmi nahin hain* [Muslims are not among us]. Thus Muslims have become new outsiders in Indian politics.

Do you agree with the view that Modi has failed to fulfil his promises to ensure "development" for all after coming to power? According to his own government's statistics, 308 communal incidents have been reported in the country in the first six months of this year, of which 56 have taken place in Uttar Pradesh alone.

Unlike the Congress-led UPA—which had the principle of social justice and welfare of the people, despite that fact that it was not properly implemented during its 10 years of rule—the BJP rule, in contrast, follows low intensity communalism against Muslims. But one should keep in mind that the old Modi is gone and his dirty work is being executed by his right-hand and BJP president Amit Shah. While Manmohan, Chidambaram and Montek were the face of growth and the Gandhi family that of social justice, Modi is now the mascot of good governance, keeping silent on the communal issue while Amit Shah will do the opposite. These two contradictory things will operate simultaneously in Indian politics.

Will you attribute the unprecedented victory of the BJP in the General Election, particularly in UP, to its ability to incite and maintain a situation of communal tension?

Apart from the saffronisation of lower castes, there are other reasons as well. Modi came to power riding on an anti-Congress wave. I will explain to you why I call it a positive move. This anti-Congress wave was founded on the solid grounds of demands for more welfare measures. It was a discontent against inflation and unemployment. Amid this condition of unrest, it is Modi who succeeded in convincing the masses that he could deliver. During the UPA rule we witnessed the facelessness of neoliberalism as nobody owned the responsibility for crisis, as a result of price rise, unemployment and agrarian stagnation.

Even the UPA Government, instead of addressing the crisis, attributed them to foreign factors. Even the Gandhi family failed to take responsibility and provide relief to the masses. In the wake of this, the RSS pinned their trust in Modi and embarked on a plan for mass mobilisation. The RSS meticulously planned everything and did a detailed study of each constituency. There is even a talk that the BJP spent 300 crore to field dummy Muslim candidates to divide Muslim votes. That is why the BJP was able to bag 282 seats with just 31 per cent vote share. Besides, the rise of Ann Hazare and the Aam Aadmi Party also contributed to the victory of Modi. I have been long arguing that the anti-corruption movement of Anna Hazare and AAP, which is essentially a middle class movement, rhetorically talked of majoritarian language with no real agenda. In the 1970s the JP movement also did the same thing but they have all not heeded the fact that the source of corruption lies in many factors, such as the structure of political economy, nepotism and caste network in bureaucracy and the nature of economic reforms of our country. There was a deep sense of cynicism among the middle class and this brought them closer to Modi.

Are you worried about the report of media that there is a possibility of the BJP to maintain communal tension for electoral gains in the upcoming by-elections in western UP and the state assembly election in 2017? In other words, what is the relationship between polls and communal polarisation?

As I mentioned above the riots are engineered by the BJP for electoral gains and it is likely to pursue the same policy. But the most important aspect is why has the BJP been successful in its plan? Answer to this lies in the fact that it enjoys considerable acceptance not only among its traditional voters like Brahmins and Banias but also among an increasing section of subalterns.

There are the incidents of communal fissures between Dalits and Muslims (Azamgarh), Sikhs and Muslims (Saharanpur) in UP. How do you look at this?

The RSS fuels anti-Muslim feelings among Sikhs using the memory of Partition. As for Dalits versus Muslims conflicts, I have dwelt on it earlier that it is due to entrenched caste psyche and rightward shift of lower caste politics. Today there is little incentive to be secular. Even the secular forces are only concerned about their own issues and they do not join a cross-sectional front. For example, how many Dalits are there to talk about Muslim issues? How many Muslims are raising the issues of Adivasis? There is a need to give up this secular sectarianism.

What do you have to say about the weakening of the Bahujan Samajwadi Party?

The BSP is now working with bottom to top approach, from Bahujan to Sarvajan, while the BJP's strategy is top-down from upper caste to Dalits. In other words, the BSP started with Dalits and ended up with the upper caste, while the BJP journeyed from upper castes and reached Dalits. Unlike the 1980s and the 1990s, the BSP does not have any unique ideas today. The biggest challenge before the BSP is the RSS and the BJP's ability to make an inroad among Dalits. For example, the recent trend shows that a large section of urban Dalits voted for Modi.

Apart from Modi, Akhilesh Yadav's government in UP has also come in for sharp criticism for its failure to check the incidents of communal violence. Is it not a paradox that the SP government in UP, which was given a huge mandate, particularly from Muslims and Backward Castes in the assembly election to fulfil secular agendas, has failed to arrest the incidents of anti-Muslim violence in UP, particularly in areas of Kosi Kalaan, Bareilly, Faizabad, Meerut, Saharanpur, Shabhal, Shamli, Masuri, Ghaziabad, etc.?

The secular parties, like the SP, are involved in secular sectarianism. While the BJP eyed majority Hindu votes, the SP also saw communal tension in UP as electorally beneficial because Muslims have been its traditional voters. The Akhilesh government wanted to keep the conflict small so that a sense of insecurity would draw naturally Muslims to the SP but things went out of control and the fire of communal tensions engulfed large parts of western UP.

The opposition Congress is today attacking the Modi Government for inciting as many as 600 incidents of communal riots. Don't you think that the oldest party of India was also not serious about the prevention of communal violence when it was in power at the Centre for 10 years? Do you support the view that had it been so, Prevention of Communal and Targeted Violence would have been long passed?

The Congress was interested to pass the Anti-Communal Violence Bill but it is also a fact that it cannot go for hard secularism as it fears that it will be seen as anti-Hindu with a Christian party president in Sonia Gandhi at the top. That is why it does want to appear to be pro-Muslim and it fears that the talk of Muslim welfare will consolidate Hindu majority votes against it. This is the dilemma of secular parties. How much do they want to pursue inclusive policies for Muslims without polarising politics?

As you said that Muslims are the new subaltern group of India? What evidence do you have to support this claim?

As a new subaltern of the country, Muslims are marginalised in all three spheres, social, economic and political. They remain socially ostracised, economically deprived and politically unrepresented. Even the other marginalised social groups like Dalits and OBCs are not deprived in all three spheres. Muslims are becoming an easy target of even those who are placed at the bottom of the Hindu caste hierarchy. I, therefore, support 10 to 12 per cent of Muslim reservation. As far as the opposition that Muslims cannot be given reservation, I do not find any substantive point in this. On the basis of concrete social backwardness, they deserve affirmative actions. I also do not quite agree with the argument of the Pasmanda Movement that Ashraf Muslims cannot be included into the ambit of reservation. To address their concerns, there can be the creamy layer cap, like OBCs, among Muslims. Besides, there is a need to create a middle class among Muslims

Published in *twocircles.net*, August 20, 2014.

37

The Rightward Shift in Dalit Politics

Where are Dalit politics heading in India today? They seem to have come a full circle from the agenda of 'annihilation of caste' to 'secularisation of caste', and conversion from Hinduism to actively claiming the Hindu identity, as is evident from the spate of communal riots that we have witnessed in Uttar Pradesh in the last few months, which have been primarily between the Dalits and the Muslims. The dynamics in rural Dalit politics seem to have moved from challenging the upper castes to finding acceptance and becoming a part of the majoritarian polity that is under construction. Mobility by gaining acceptance looks far more tangible, and achievable, as against the abstract and a rather 'utopian' idea of annihilating caste. This acceptance can be perceived as a mobility as well as undermining the dominance of the upper castes, in compelling them to recognise the fact that they need the Dalit support in the rural hinterlands, against the perceived aggression of the Muslims, and that they are mutually interdependent.

Dalit identity has itself internally fractured, as the issue of conflicting interests, including practice of untouchability between the various sub-castes among the Dalits is coming to the fore and gaining political articulation; there is little that can hold the identity together, as it did in the past. Further, sustained mobilisation of the Dalits by political parties such as the Congress in the past had benefited certain sub-castes within the Dalits, for various historical and sociological reasons. It is those who feel the sense of having lost out that are finding a new political space with the BJP. The case is similar with the OBCs, where mobilisation by parties such as the SP, RJD and

JD(U) benefited the dominant factions within the OBCs, such as the Yadavs and the Kurmis. Though JD(U) under Mr. Nitish Kumar made an extra effort by sub-dividing—into EBCs and MBCs—the OBCs in order to reach out to the less privileged, this nevertheless has come to be perceived to be happening within the tutelage and patronage of the dominant OBC castes that is no longer acceptable. The coming together of Mr. Lalu Prasad Yadav and Nitish Kumar is precisely to put brakes to the process of BJP weaning away the less privileged OBC castes from their fold.

Further, the larger sub-castes among the Dalits have mostly converted to Christianity and less so to Islam. The smaller sub-castes by de fault are therefore left with the option of moving within the Hindu-fold. Moreover, the vulnerability felt by smaller sub-castes, not so much from the upper castes, but from their fellow Dalit sub-castes, who eclipsed them and got relatively more benefits than them, can be made good by the assumed power of aligning with the dominant and the majority Hindu religion. The weakness of size and social backwardness is sought to be made good by accruing power in joining the majoritarian political construct. Finally, all this as a social process is being further strengthened by the change in the strategy of the BJP and the RSS, who now perceive the possibility of actively mobilising the Dalits, without losing the support base of the so-called upper castes. While the BSP attempted this strategy bottom-up by moving from the Bahujan to the Sarvajan, the BJP-RSS combine is attempting the same strategy top-down.

The story is slightly different with the urban Dalits, who moved to the cities by seeking education and benefiting from the affirmative action policies of the last four decades. The emergent 'new' middle classes from amongst these Dalit families continued to feel the pinch of caste within the anonymity of urban spaces. However, even this social group, if we go by recent poll statistics, voted for Mr. Modi in UP and Bihar and is certainly moving towards the fold of the BJP. The possibility here seems to be that the new aspirational social group amongst the Dalits wishes to be as much a part of the growth-story as the traditional upper castes. Here, it is much less of the Hindu-identity, as it is about a perceived universalism of the benefits of growth and governance. This political language also provides anonymity and ostensibly sidelines and undermines the language of caste that comes as a relief to the urban Dalit. This comes with a belief that globalisation cannot be understood with a simple-minded monolithic frame that it is neo-liberal in content but one needs to concede that it undermines caste-based labour practices, and it has opened new economic opportunities for the Dalits, unlike the local or national capital. It is this mood or constituency that Mr. Udit Raj represents in the BJP, who otherwise was a champion of conversions of Dalits from the fold of Hinduism to Buddhism, yet becomes acceptable to the BJP. It is also for this very reason that today the Dalit movement has developed as much contempt for the Left parties and left-based social mobilisation as the traditional upper-caste social elites in India and the traditional right-wing political parties such as the BJP. This is yet another growing commonality between the Right and the neo-Dalit agenda in Indian politics, which is why Udit Raj joining the BJP or Ram Vilas Paswan joining the coalition is perceived as part of a pragmatic move necessary for the current Dalit-agenda, while Arundhati Roy writing on Ambedkar is perceived as an illegitimate appropriation and worst still as 'poaching' from the outside. Here, strangely, Dalit politics uses the exclusivist Dalit identity and the need to be born a Dalit to speak of caste and Ambedkar. Earlier, in the 1970s and even the 80s the tension between Dalit and Left politics was articulated around how to draw equivalence between caste and classes, now however Dalit politics has a conflict with the very vision of the Left and the anti-capitalist agenda. This they perceive as yet another strategy of the upper castes, in the garb of Leftism, to dislodge the upper mobility of the Dalit entrepreneurs, and coming of age of 'Dalit entrepreneurs' and 'Dalit millionaires', while Ambedkar himself all along unequivocally argued against both Brahmanism and Capitalism, as twin processes that have perpetuated caste in India. The post-Ambedkarite Dalit politics, among other things, is gradually but unmistakably taking a rightward shift, this in turn would be decisive for the content and contours of democracy in India, for a long time to come.

Published in *The Hindu*, September 13, 2014.

State and Democracy

38

Why Fake Encounters

The debate, following the revelation by the CBI, in the print and electronic media has expressed strong concern and the need in a democracy to protect rule of law. It however needs to be understood that this debate on extrajudicial killings need to move beyond Gujarat and Muslims.

The case of Ishrat Jahan has to be located in the context of a growing exceptionalism within Indian democracy, and the collective failure of the state and society in finding political solutions to various issues that include the simmering discontent in Kashmir, and parts of the north-east, Maoist insurrection in central India, spread of religious extremism of various hues, protest by farmers and workers, among others.

As long as the state and society do not come to an agreement that these issues need an urgent political resolution, through dialogue and wider consultative and participatory mechanisms, Indian democracy will continue to be held to ransom to the vagaries of exceptionalism and it would increasingly be believed that securitisation of the state would be a compelling precondition for development. This, in effect, has become a vicious cycle that has been growing and widening in the last four decades.

The language of fake encounters entered the popular lexicon in India way back in the 1970s with the Vengal Rao government in Andhra Pradesh. In due course the number of allegations and demands by various civil rights organisations to investigate various alleged encounters steadily grew in number. Over time, came into existence what is again called in popular parlance as 'encounter specialists.' This was followed by vigilante groups such as the ULFA in Assam and more recently Salwa Judum in Chhattisgarh.

Alongside these modes of exceptionalism, Indian democracy has been a witness to various extra-ordinary laws such as the Tada, Pota, and Afspa. These laws consistently moved from the realm of evidence to that of intention, and preventive strike was legitimised as a necessary mode of controlling militancy and various kinds of private violence.

Extraordinary Acts such as Afspa legalised many of the practices that would otherwise stand to be deemed unconstitutional. The argument in favour of promulgating such Acts was that they were used judiciously in limited territorial jurisdiction that was declared to be a disturbed area. In other words, extraordinary laws were deemed necessary to control extraordinary situations.

Legal Justification

However, the logic of exceptionalism never seems to remain exceptional but always has the propensity to generalise itself because it comes to supplant political debate and public reasoning. In fact debating the situation, and raising the possibility of a dialogue itself comes to be perceived in due course as sedition. It thereby opens up the possibility that there could be enough public and legal justification that extra-ordinary provisions should in fact be made part of regular law. This shift in India took place with the constitution of the Justice Malimath Committee on reforms of criminal justice system, which submitted its recommendations in 2003 and is still pending before Parliament.

In essence, the report collapses the distinction between extra-ordinary and ordinary law. Some of its recommendations include replacement of the provision of guilty beyond reasonable doubt be replaced by 'the court is convinced that it is true'; removal of distinction between 'cognisable offence' and 'non-cognisable offence'; withdrawal of the Right to Silence of the accused by 'amending the code to provide for appropriate inferences from the silences of the accused; the confession before a superintendent of police or a higher ranking official should be made admissible as evidence before the courts. The committee justifies its recommendations on the basis of the observation that the criminal justice system has failed to deter criminals and has been found wanting in its rate of conviction.

Alongside, the extension of the scope of exceptionalism, comes the normalisation of the use of such methods. While these methods are often justified as necessary to contain earlier dacoits, more recently religious extremism, terrorism, Maoists, and militant organisations of various kinds, in due course they have the potential to be used in various kinds of social conflicts and not just against militants or what we refer to as 'extremists'.

This danger is more than palpable when we view cases such as Ghulam Rasool, a journalist working with a popular Telugu daily *Udayam* was killed in an alleged encounter in 2003, after being branded as a Naxalite, while the journalist association claimed that he was in fact investigating illegal land dealings; There was very little outrage that was expressed by the collective conscience of the society, since these practices had become normalised.

It is the potential of such normalisation of the extra-judicial and extraordinary laws that should worry any healthy democracy. This generalisation appears contingent but it in reality is compulsive in nature and sweeping in its scope. Collectively it is possible to arrest such generalisation and normalisation of exceptionalism, only when citizens in a democracy are willing to deliberate social and political causes for rise of various kinds of disturbances in a democracy. It is in being willing to speak reason and listen that we become champions of democracy, and not in promulgating a state of exceptionalism in the name of protecting democracy.

Published in the *Deccan Herald*, July 30, 2013.

39

Indian Democracy: Emerging Threats

Democracy as a form of governance and a way of life seems to be in peril and requires a serious rethinking within the South Asian geo-politics. Pakistan turned to military dictatorship and recently, monarchical rule has been re-imposed in Nepal. How safe and complacent can we afford to be about democratic practices in India? Although India has come to be recognised as the largest working democracy with an ostensibly smooth election process, the underlying currents and some of the growing trends might just be the revealing signposts highlighting the tenuousness of the foundations required for a healthy democracy.

To begin with, the nature of the state and economy is changing fast. There is a perceptible decline of the centrality of the agrarian and even the industrially productive classes, replaced by a meteoric rise of a class of middlemen, brokers and contractors (both liquor and civil) who thrive on muscle power, corrupting the officials and brazen violation of institutional norms. This rising class has captured the formal institutions and entered into a strong nexus with the various organs of the government, including the police. For instance, in Andhra Pradesh the leading political parties consist of a sizeable proportion of liquor and civil contractors, which explains the hue and cry over the contracts for the irrigation projects and also the recent attempt to pass a government order allowing for the opening of any number of bars in villages with a population of over 25,000. So is the controversy surrounding the constructions around the Taj Mahal. The democratic space in the civil society for organisations and activists struggling for various issues across the board is rapidly declining and instead there is a rising "uncivil society" marked by rampant mafiaisation beginning with small time goondas (who in course of time become important political leaders) involved in collection of haftas, to private armed groups encouraged and backed by the state, such as the SULFA in Assam, gradually generating a fear psychosis that makes society at large silent and indifferent to social issues. The nexus these groups are entering into with the traditional elite is grossly disturbing. Awarding rape as a punishment for opting for inter-caste marriage by a Khap Panchayat in Meerut not long ago is some evidence for this consolidation.

The democratic space for institutional, spontaneous or organised activity against these threats is fast declining as potential symbols are collapsing. Judiciary has over time become increasingly conservative; traditional symbols such as those of the religious heads, which at least stood for asceticism are mired in sexual scandals and corruption; activists of the stature of Anna Hazare are easily framed pushing society at large into ambiguity, indifference and pessimism. The crisis, it seems, is hardly acknowledged, leave alone attempts to address it. Instead, political parties wish to circumvent the brewing crisis with vacuous "India shining" campaigns that offer a false sense of pride by inciting effortless "cartographic nationalism". Military solutions for genuine social and economic grievances get renewed legitimacy and the excesses committed get absolved and the rule of law violated with impunity. The rape of Manorama in Manipur being a case in point. These are the same forces that encourage parochialism while projecting nations to be "global villages". Cities that once proudly claimed to be cosmopolitan are becoming highly parochial and this is reflected in campaigns against the "outsiders" in Maharashtra or the lobbying against Hindi and English movies in Karnataka.

The media, on its part, is increasingly resorting to sensationalism so as to cater to the ongoing mood. While entertainment value of news has outstripped other priorities in the electronic media; news dailies seem to be competing with one another in bringing page 3 stuff to their front pages. They even aid in the process of leading sports personalities being reduced, at best, from symbols of achievement and hard work to crude commercial agents, and, at worst, into sex symbols. As a consequence, the youth of the nation are left with no worthwhile role models to emulate.

Educational institutions are becoming self-claimed "centres of excellence" and centres for professional education, which is actually a euphemism for encouraging socially insulated education where social conflicts and problems are reduced to mere "technical issues". Not to mention growing ideological intolerance and meaningless bickering, failure to generate healthy work ethic and critical discourses with campus life for students becoming increasingly depoliticised, and easy compromise on autonomy and transparency of the educational institutions with research being conditioned by the "priority areas" of the donors.

The family as an institution is in deep crisis. There seems to be no effective alternative emerging that could accommodate and stand for values of compassion, sharing, and selflessness. Often there is ambiguity amongst the progressive forces in negotiating with "traditions". The entire baggage of traditions and local practices is left untapped by democratic forces only to be appropriated by monolithic interpretations that allow free play, for instance, for the far-right organisations such as the Durga Vahinis to conservatively politicise women around the symbols of 'Durga' and 'Sita'.

The market seems to be singularly the most effective institution attracting and influencing the lifestyles allowing for a free play of ego and hedonism, a false sense of mobility, and momentary gratification through the use of latest gadgets be it the fancy mobiles, handycams or laptops and palmtops. Needless to say, it is making life extremely insecure with contractualisation of jobs, withdrawal of social welfare policies such as pension for the aged and replacing it with uncertain investments in mutually beneficial bonds, and increasingly pushing vulnerable groups such as women and children into long working hours and hazardous work conditions. Corporatisation with solely profit-making motive has affected across the sectors, beginning with education, health to agriculture. Rising controversies around the consequences of using Monsanto seeds or excessive usage of ground water in Kerala or even more condemnable attempts to privatise rivers in Madhya Pradesh are only glaring examples of much deeper changes that would adversely affect in times to come. Technology is coming to replace not only the 'strong tie' inter personal relations but also define the very identity and purpose of life. Meaningful leisure is a grave casualty confused with trivialised entertainment and social engagements. Pursuit of interests without immediate benefits—something which Bertrand Russell pointed out as imperative for the "Conquest of Happiness"—and carrying larger social concerns seem to find no place in the emerging scheme of things.

This increasing 'one-dimensionality' of the society is a serious cause for concern and a formidable impediment for a healthy democracy. Herbert Marcuse, writing in the context of America, had warned in the early 1960s that 'one-dimensionality' is an indication for the rising nexus between conservative forces of various hues and that humanity will have to pay heavily in its attempt to wriggle out of it. Perhaps nothing could be more appropriate than this to help us understand some of the contemporary transformation that India is undergoing at present.

Published in *The Sentinel*, June 15, 2005.

40

Regional Parties and Regionalising Democracy

Among many other features of democracy in India is the growing federalisation with the rise of regional parties. Regional parties, which sprang into prominence in India after the collapse of the Congress rule in 1967, began to represent regional diversity in terms of economic needs and cultural aspirations.

They were also the representative political forces of regional bourgeoisie that began to take shape from agrarian surplus after the Green Revolution, as against the national and global capital flows.

They have steadily played a bigger role in national politics though they repeatedly failed to provide stable governments at the Centre, whenever they attempted to form a 'Third Front'. The failure to form stable alliances is representative of the federal structure with unitary features, where the regional parties seem to be able to come together in a stable coalition only while rallying around national parties, either Congress or the BJP.

The question this time around is, will the general elections 2014 be any different? Will regional parties such as the BJD, RJD, TMC, SP, BSP, AIADMK, and TDP, manage a Third Front? Or would they prefer to join one of the coalitions led by a national party? One of the reasons for repeated failures of forging and managing the Third Front has been the failure of regional parties to think and present an agenda at the national level, and also the failure to strike an alternative social and economic programme that is different from the national parties.

Reforms by Stealth

This process has become all the more difficult with a near-consensus on economic reforms and carrying out 'reforms by stealth', at the national as well as regional levels. This is not to say that there are no competing or conflicting interests that these parties represent but just that they have preferred simply not to represent their constituencies.

Perhaps, one of the initial trends in contrast to this near-consensus model has been the recent protest by various regional parties with regard to the issue of FDI in the retail sector. Most of the regional parties, including the SP, TMC and BSP spoke a different language of protecting the 'small traders' in their states against the giant incursions by multinational brands such as the Walmart.

Similarly, regional parties need to represent agriculture. Many states such as Andhra Pradesh, Maharashtra, Bihar, Madhya Pradesh, etc are facing acute agrarian crisis, which has resulted in farmers' suicides. However, in the changing dynamics, the regional parties began to play a different tune of allowing corporate agriculture, with the introduction of Monsanto seeds, expensive fertilizers, cash crops, crop insurance, and other such market-oriented moves in order to facilitate the transfer of agricultural sector from the local to the global.

In Andhra Pradesh, for instance, Y.S. Rajsekhar Reddy came to power in 2004 and again in 2009 with a series of welfare measures for the farmers and other marginalised sections of the rural hinterlands, which included free electricity, free transportation for the farmers to sell their produce, Arogyashree health scheme for the rural poor, housing, among others. It is a paradox that a regional party like the TDP began to represent global capital and adopted the economic model presented by the World Bank, while a national party like the Congress came back with an agrarian agenda.

This interchange of their historic roles is the result of a super-imposed economic model of growth. It was again Congress that pressed for the recent Land Acquisition Bill (2012), invoking the role of panchayats in acquiring land for the purpose of industry, while parties such as the CPI (M) lost power in West Bengal for its forceful acquisition of land, although they had represented the interests of the peasants for the last three decades, including carrying out land reforms in the 1960s. This is again symptomatic of the role-reversal from land reforms to land acquisition.

Quality Education

Along with agriculture, regional parties also need to take up education as their second most important agenda. Mostly, when agriculture does well, the demand for good education goes up. Providing quality schooling will propel inter-generational mobility and also partially address the inequalities across caste, class, gender and the rural-urban divide. Regional parties could take up the issue of the 'common neighbourhood schooling system' like in the US.

Under this system, the government should ensure near-similar quality schooling across the state and make it mandatory that all those residing in a particular geographical limit need to go to the same school. The recent Right to Education Act has provided 25 per cent preferential admission in corporate schools to children coming from economically weak backgrounds.

Health is another pressing need in many parts of India. The recent debate on compulsory one-year posting for government junior doctors is a right move in that direction. The discourse of 'youth' in India has been centred on an urban imagination, and the debate around 'demographic dividend' also has urban youth aspiring global opportunities, which has however missed out on rural youth. It is part of this discourse that junior doctors recently protested against mandatory rural-postings.

However, it would be pertinent to push a system of mandatory rural posting for many other professions, including teachers, engineers, and lawyers, among others. Wider role for regional parties is by definition healthy for democracy, provided these parties represent the diversity they belong to rather than follow-suit the national and global models of development.

Published in the *Deccan Herald*, March 16, 2014.

41

New Regional Parties: Praja Rajyam Party and YSR (Congress)

When the Congress, under Y.S. Rajasekhara Reddy, returned to power in Andhra Pradesh in 2009, it was believed that the party would be a force to reckon with for a long time. But YSRs death in a helicopter crash in September 2009 dramatically changed the state's political environment. In less than two years, the Congress seems to have lost its hold on the politics of the region and that, in turn, is leading to new developments that are redefining electoral equations.

The YSR Congress, a splinter group from the Congress, was formed by YSR's disgruntled son Jaganmohan Reddy. Then the newly formed Praja Rajyam Party by actor Chiranjeevi merged with the Congress. There has also been the revival of the struggle for a separate state of Telangana that YSR had managed to contain when he was at the helm. The demand for Telangana created a new political phenomenon: of politicians expressing allegiance to their region as against their party. In Andhra Pradesh now, the region you belong to is more important than the party or ideology you represent.

In order to survive politically and get the mandate of the electorate, legislators across parties are compelled to indicate that they would preserve the interests of the region they come from, even in defiance of party diktats. This conflict—between loyalty to the region and to the party—is further complicated by loosening the grip of national leadership over regional leaders and local dynamics. This was evident in the recent crisis in Karnataka as well where the central leadership of the BJP had little or no say in the way B.S. Yeddyurappa made his exit as CM or in the way his successor was chosen. This weakening hold of national leadership is a reversal of the political process introduced by Indira Gandhi, who had a direct connect with the electorate and who undermined local leadership with her interference in state politics.

State-level leaders often emerge from a reworking of caste equations and by imagining policies that are popular with the electorate. In Andhra Pradesh,YSR had rolled out a large number of welfare policies for the poor, including free housing, subsidised rice and special transport facilities in rural areas for farmers to take their produce to the market. These appealed to various sections of the electorate. It is this legacy of YSR that Jagan is attempting to appropriate. He has emerged as a force, and this should be seen in the context of a debilitated Congress. The resignation letters submitted by its legislators from the Telangana region had weakened the party. Now, 27 more MLAs have submitted their resignations to the speaker and they are set to join Jagan's YSR Congress.

The Congress, in order to stop Jagan's surge,found a way forward by discrediting the legacy and image of YSR after the CBI filed an FIR against the former chief minister in an ongoing investigation into the allegation that his family has amassed assets disproportionate to known sources of income. This, the Congress believes, will also strengthen its claim of fighting corruption. But the legislators' bid to join Jagan has complicated the survival of political parties.

Jagan's hold over the electorate is restricted to Rayalaseema and the Andhra region. In fact, when he attempted to take out his "Odarpu Yatra" into Telangana, his entourage was attacked by students. In order to counter Jagan's popularity in the Andhra region, the Congress carried out negotiations with Chiranjeevi, which fructified in the Praja Rajyam Party, which managed to get 27 per cent of votes in the last assembly elections, merging with the Congress on the eve of Rajiv Gandhi's birth anniversary. The alliance might give some comfort to the Congress.

But Telangana is a more complicated case. In spite of its silence on the issue of Telangana, the Telugu Desam Party still retains formidable support from backward castes. The electoral conflict in the Telangana region is now primarily between the TDP and the Telangana Rashtra Samithi (TRS), with minimal prospects for the Congress, given the way it handled the demand for a separate state.

The TDP is already making noises about introducing a no-trust motion in the assembly and N. Chandrababu Naidu, in the backdrop of the investigations against Jagan, is on anti-corruption mode and planning even to go on a hunger strike in support of Anna Hazare's campaign.

What is certain in this changing scenario is that local dynamics will have a greater influence in state politics, especially in the absence of tall national leaders.

Published in *The Indian Express*, August 26, 2011.

42

The Uncanny Indian Voter

The results from three of the assembly seats in the by-election in Uttarakhand, where Congress won them all, came as a surprise to the observers and analysts of Indian elections. Just when we were settling down to talk about the way the Modi-led government was performing, the Indian voter seems to be already changing gears and posing new questions as to how to make sense of the choices and the patterns that emerge and change course in electoral processes. The relation between the voter and the politician and political parties seems to be one between Tom and Jerry, each trying to outplay the other. The repertoire of tricks that the Indian voter has performed has kept the political parties on their toes, and they need to come up with new strategies and agendas to serve the economic needs, political choices and cultural appetite. To begin with, elections in India have witnessed relatively large voter-turn out (well over 60%), just when we were beginning to discuss the apathy in the political system, endemic suspicion of the politician as a public figure and the capacity of the political parties to mobilise the common voter. Even as the voters have expressed their inability to get substantive benefits from the ruling elites, and complain about rampant corruption across all the parties, they have turned out in bigger numbers to beat this mood. The formalism of the electoral process- electoralism- is supplanted by the enthusiastic participation of the average voter. Even in states such as Chhattisgarh that have witnessed abject neglect, and sustained presence of the Maoists, who have been giving an all-out call to boycott elections, the voter turn-out has been very high. Added to this, when economic reforms began to be implemented and the policy frame of all political parties began to increasingly look very similar, the voter changed gears and moved from registering anti-incumbency to pro-incumbency and returned same parties to the government in any number of states. From Delhi, Chhattisgarh, Madhya Pradesh to Andhra Pradesh that was recently bifurcated. From bargaining benefits by voting-out the existing government, the voter found a more sustainable bargain in voting-in the incumbent governments. They managed through this a significant shift in the policy frame of all the major political parties. All parties that began with an exclusive growth-centric rhetoric, led by the Congress, in 1999, began to campaign and contest elections on welfare agenda by 2004 and this trend got further entrenched in the elections in 2009 that Congress fought, not on growth but on the basis of implementing MGNREGA. The Congress attempted to repeat this feat by formulating a massive Food Security Bill in 2014, yet the voter chose to vote them out and elect a government led by Modi that hardly spoke about new welfare programmes, instead focused on 'maximum governance and minimum government'. This led to a debate whether the voter is no longer prepared for 'doles' but needs economic opportunities/ empowerment and dignity. While they were disillusioned with Congress for poor implementation and leakages in the welfare programmes, they chose a government that promised higher growth and better governance. Even in this the voter made an interesting differentiation between the party and the personality. The vote was for Modi and not BJP. They felt the BJP is as ineffective as the Congress but it was on Modi that they ostensibly laid their trust on, since he was prepared to take responsibility. In the facelessness that neoliberal order presents, Modi was the face that was visible. This could well be the reason why voters were angry with the Gandhis and not that they have rejected 'dynasty rule', as it is often made out to be.

Even as we are settling in to understand the effects and contours of the 'Modi wave' and the 'Modi phenomenon' the post-poll surveys in Delhi suggested that BJP might not perform well or keep their vote-share intact if there were to be elections for Delhi Assembly. Among other choices, the voter has consistently made a difference in voting for general elections as against the assembly elections. Even in states that witnessed simultaneous elections for the parliament and the assembly, they voted in a different measure. This was clear with the rise and the fall of AAP. While they came to power in a dramatic fashion, they suffered a whitewash in parliamentary elections that followed within a short duration. AAP is now ruing finding reasons for this sudden disillusionment with their politics. The idea that giving up power, the way they did in Delhi, seem to have not had the desired effect of impressing the voter who otherwise accuses the politician and political parties of being 'power hungry'. Instead, they read Kejriwal's choice as opportunism, and inability to govern and running away from the responsibility and trust imposed in him and his party. BJP therefore is in two minds whether or not to stake claim to form the government in Delhi. Will it be seen as taking responsibility, or will it be seen as trying to benefit from the existing mood, and taking advantage of the voter. What are its long-term effects on the party and the image that Mr.Modi so carefully cultivated?

It is, perhaps, for the first time that we are witnessing a party that has come with a massive majority to be under pressure within such a short duration. This majority is also significant because it is caused a tectonic shift in the electoral pattern. Just when the pandits were writing off national parties and single-party governments in the centre and declared that the coalition governments are here to stay, the voter turned in a single party with a massive majority. However, there is already a talk of the waning Modi-effect. Are parties beginning to wilt under the hype that they created? This also seemed to be the case with AAP. The euphoria generated died out rather quickly. While the Congress seemed to be a party with ideas and churned out new welfare policies, but failed to implement them effectively, BJP that promised effective implementation seems to have no new ideas, at least till now. The big picture of governing a country of this size and diversity is certainly missing in what we witnessed over the last two months. Whether it was Mr. Jaitley's budget, or Sushma Swaraj's management of foreign affairs, or Mr. Naidu's statements on urban development that are sought to be made good by more accountability and stricter monitoring of officers in his ministry. Modi himself seems to be struggling to find a new persona that is different from his aggressive posturing during the campaign days. The question realiy is how would BJP counter the hype that it created? Would it be able to sustain the promised shift from sectarian mobilisation to 'pure' governance? Or are we set to witness a combination of high-intensity growth policy with low-intensity communalism? Anointment of Amit Shah as party president and Mr. Ram Madhav, a pracharak and long-term spokesperson of the RSS that always claimed to be only a cultural organisation, as its general secretary could be some signposts towards this incumbent combination by the BJP. The speed and alacrity with which the voter is engaging with the political process, the politician and parties certainly need ideas and policies that can effectively make a difference to their everyday lives.

Published in *The Hindu*, August 5, 2014.

43

Politics Without Opposition

The new political dispensation is caught between two visible political discourses that do not look compatible at the moment but the political experiment to find a middle ground that obliterates the tension between them is on. The conflict is between development and governance on the one hand and communalism on the other, where the former is ostensibly universal and all-inclusive, while the latter is divisive, discriminatory and sectarian.

The possible way to balance this is to browbeat the religious minorities in terms of their claims to an independent cultural identity and visible religious practices; thus the announcement by the Rashtriya Swayamsevak Sangh (RSS) chief that "all Indians are Hindus" or Narendra Modi's refusal to wear the skullcap, while making appeals to Muslims and attempts to reach out to them to be a part of the new development agenda. Therefore, it is important to claim that Muslims in Gujarat are better off than under any other government that claims to be secular. This resonates with the slogan that the Bharatiya Janata Party (BJP) went to the polls with— "Sabka Saath Sabka Vikas."

Onus on Minorities

Cultural subjugation is sought to be made good through economic integration. This trade-off also lays the onus on Muslims to carry out internal reforms within their community to be eligible to be a part of the modern education and economic opportunities available due to ongoing market reforms and efficient governance. Here the claims to a separate cultural identity begin to look out of place since it can be very easily perceived not only as anti-development but also as anti-national in its "refusal" to get integrated, thereby becoming obstructionist to modern development.

This further leads to the BJP's claims that while it is prepared to integrate the religious minorities, it is they who are unprepared to do so. If there is tension between communities or between the discourse of the government and the minority community, the blame can squarely be laid on the latter. In this new mode, the universalism and integrative capacity of the development discourse sits well with the homogenisation of the cultural sphere, and therefore with the project of radical Hinduisation. Further, secular discourse here signifying protective policies and social welfare schemes for specific communities can easily be made to look like appeasement and unsustainable doles, in place of an efficient and robust economy. Secularism is therefore an outmoded discourse of the Nehruvian era that holds back economic advancement.

This logic however does not or cannot be limited to the religious minorities but needs to necessarily be inclusive of the Other Backward Classes (OBC), Dalits and also tribals. In only such an inclusion can the discourse look universal and all encompassing. It is in order to make this adjustment that the BJP has to reach out to OBCs, Dalits and tribals. It is this project which is visible in the anointment of Mr. Modi as the prime ministerial candidate of the BJP, signifying a process of the Bahujanisation of the Hindu right-wing party. The BJP, as is widely believed, is the first party to have taken upon itself to make an OBC the Prime Minister, unlike all other mainstream political parties, including the Left parties. Representation trumps all other forms of pursuing social justice. It is to further this very mode of pursuing a new kind of politics that Mr. Bhagwat has recently and for the first time publicly supported the policy of reservations for the Scheduled Castes and Scheduled Tribes at an event in Delhi marked by the release of three volumes on the history of three Scheduled Castes that included the Balmikis, the Khatiks and the Charmakars.

Equality is Alien

These volumes have been authored by Vijay Sonkar Shastri, a

Dalit and a former MLA with the BJP from Uttar Pradesh. They broadly make the claim that there was no untouchability in the Vedic ages and it was a later day practice that came into existence with the "Muslim invaders." The volumes further claim that while the Khatiks were originally Brahmins, the Balmikis and the Charmakars were Khastriyas. Since these were the warrior communities which refused to convert to Islam, they were assigned menial jobs such as scavenging, dealing with leather and sweeping. Some of them were prisoners of war who were forced to do manual work and forcefully segregated from the rest of the society, and thereby introduced to the hitherto unknown practice of untouchability.

The volume on Charmakars claims that the word "chamar" is an Arabic word, denoting those dealing with leather work. It was with the advent of the British, colonial rule and the process of codification, that the practice of untouchability against the depressed classes came to be rigid. The volumes make a further claim that Buddhism, Sikhism and Jainism are all variants of Hinduism; therefore, there were no forced conversions in any of these religions; in fact, even Brahmins willingly converted to these "forms" of practising Hinduism. The volumes make a further plea to write a more detailed history of the tribals also (which the RSS has already taken up). As these were the communities that also resisted attempts at conversion but were unable to resist the might of the "Muslim invaders," they chose to run away into the forests in order to protect themselves. It is these Hindu communities that began to inhabit forests that are the tribes of today and who have been deprived of the benefits of modern development.

The volumes suggest an interesting way out of the current logjam. They argue that the idea of equality is alien to our culture as it promotes antagonism, and what our civilisation is based on is cultural diversity. Therefore, what we need is not equality — Samantha, but Samarastha—social harmony. The volumes further suggest that by repeatedly referring to certain castes as being Dalits, we only further reinforce their demeaned status. Instead, we need to look at the history of how they have come to be one and pull them out. Therefore, we need to preserve our cultural and community differences but also fight against untouchability, resonating the Gandhian strategy (which partly explains the newfound love of the current dispensation for Gandhi). We also need to celebrate the glorious legends of/in each of the castes in order to restore to them their original pride in Hindu society. These volumes clearly reflect a move towards a de-Brahmanising of the Hindu religion by finding a place of pride for Dalit castes, while blaming the Muslim rulers and not the Hindu sacred scripts or ritual hierarchy or other Brahmanical practices.

New Opportunities

While development and governance promise to be inclusive of everyone including the tribals and also Muslims—even if they are reminded against brandishing their religious symbols as that alone is arguably the cause of communal tensions—a de-Brahmanised Hinduisation that talks of Samarastha is sought to be inclusive of all caste groups.

The recent shift in leadership in the BJP is a pointer to this, and undoubtedly presents new opportunities to the caste groups that were perhaps kept at some distance in the past by the BJP that was known as the Brahmin-Bania party. It was in this context that the Dalit-Bahujan scholar Kancha Ilaiah, in a recent interview, remarked that "if Modi starts the liberation of backward classes, castes and tribes, he can become a cult-figure for backwards" and can be comparable to Abraham Lincoln. With no effective imagination outside modern development and growth, and little reason to have effective opposition to a more representative and de-Brahmanised Hindusim pursued by the BJP-RSS combine, there is a clear possibility of moving towards a new kind of politics without opposition. There is no doubt that the current dispensation is being reasonable in expecting itself to be playing a long innings.

Published in *The Hindu*, October 9, 2014.
(Co-authored with Sudhir Kumar Suthur)

44

Hindu Rashtra and Secular Sectarianism

Political imagination in India has come to a standstill, aiding and abetting the construction of a homogenised cultural and political sphere. The roots of this exist not merely in the rightwing political imagination of a Hindu Rashtra but they also lie in the secular sectarianism pursued by secular, democratic and progressive political formations. Secular sectarianism of the feminists, Dalits, Left and religious minorities has, over a period, ghettoised communities and advanced a sectarian political imagination, leading to a political dead-end that they now find difficult to negotiate with. Cumulatively, they all seem to have contributed to a shrinking political imagination that has in turn handsomely contributed to the rise of the rightwing politics. Feminist politics in India was silenced with the demand for the Uniform Civil Code being made by the rightwing forces, unable to negotiate the competing demands between women's rights and that of the religious minorities, after the Shah Bano Case. It is a puzzle as to why they did not proceed along the lines of equating gendered practices in all the religions, whether against the Hadith or the Manusmrithi both of which, for instance, sanctioned segregation of women and considered them to be impure during the menstrual cycle, along with all other practices that placed women as less than equal to men. In fact, it was Ambedkar who argued that it is only Dalits and women who face untouchability, due to religious sanctions.

Similarly, the Dalit politics in India moved from Ambedkar as a philosopher, who was chief architect of the Constitution, to a claim that he belongs to Dalits alone. In the 1970s the demand was Ambedkar and Phule be introduced in university syllabi and taught by all in order to understand caste. Now the demand is nobody other than Dalits have the right to write and talk of Ambedkar. Similarly, earlier the idea was all dispossessed social groups are Dalits, irrespective of their caste, today even the progressive and democratic individuals and organisations are reduced to the caste they are born into; a new kind of *homo sacer*- as bare caste beings. This shift to a narrower interpretation of anti-caste imagery leads to social justice shrinking to (political) representation, where even if it is the rightwing political organisations such as the BJP or RSS that provide for an opportunity it should be taken as an opportunity for mobility that was otherwise denied to the Dalits for centuries. Today, the case for this has grown stronger with the RSS advancing a more de-Brahmanised mode of Hinduisation, in the sense of providing for leadership for individuals from the Dalit-Bahujan communities. The Dalit politics however have ceased to question as to whatever happened to forging a Bahujan Samaj, along with the OBCs and the Muslims, if they were to consider the opportunities provided by the rightwing political mobilisation as justified mobility towards undoing demeaned social status. At a more philosophical level, Brahmanism at its core is a social system that creates and perpetuates sectarianism, and therefore one wonders if a form of politics and mobility that comes with it which does not undermine sectarianism continues to reproduce Brahamanical practices. This in fact was the critique against the Left that it continues to practise Brahamanical hegemony in its sectarian tendencies, that got reflected in its inability to take up the question of caste and religion, apart from its political sectarianism vis-à-vis other political formations including many shades of left-based mobilisation itself. Mobility with dignity can be accrued only in questioning sectarianism in all its manifold forms.

This is also similar with the secular discourse regarding minority rights in India. It not only assumed Muslims and other religious minorities to be homogeneous but also articulated their concerns disconnected from other political discourses in a democracy, mentally and spatially ghettoising them into a segregated social group. For instance, Muslim political organisations could have talked not only about the witch-hunt against the Muslims from Azamgarh and encounter killings in Batla House but also about the same kind of exceptionalism being practised against tribals in Chhattisgarh and racial profiling of citizens from Northeast India. In the same breath, it would be incumbent to speak of the plight of Hindus in Baluchistan and Bangladesh, as much as the rights of Kashmiri Pundits who lost their homes. It is important to conjoin the rights of Muslims with questioning the views of Mr.Gilani on Hindu religious minorities and women in Kashmir. Citizenship as a political practice is instantiated in the right to speak for others, not in speaking just for one's own self. This becomes important also in a context where neoliberalism has in a very substantive sense undermined empathy for others, and fraternity and solidarity of all kinds.

Indian democracy that is otherwise considered to be a success story within the postcolonial nations of the world, built its foundations on secular sectarianism of various kinds. This was previously typified as the 'Congress System', where different and conflicting social groups were accommodated within the same political party. This accommodation however, retained the social status of the groups as they stood into an umbrella formation. It is this politics of forming a coalition of social groups without any sustained attempt to forge inter-sectional dialogue that is now visibly unworkable and has led to a sharp decline in the electoral prospects of the Congress. It is this very strategy of maintaining a centrist polity that has gradually shifted rightwards through replicating the same strategy of forging a status-quoist coalition but for a different purpose—of realising a Hindu Rashtra—by the rightwing political formations. This decline was made even more pronounced by the simultaneous decline of the left parties that have found themselves in a political landscape that can best be typified as a 'no mans land'.

The way forward really seems to be in opening up internal dialogue within the communities as across them. These will have to necessarily go together. This will include raising difficult questions such as masculinity within anti-caste movements that time and again attract them towards far-right groups like the

Shiv Sena, communal sentiments and inward looking philosophy of the Muslims reflected in ideas of Jihad or in considering non-Muslims as Kafirs, classism among urban feminists that precludes a more nuanced understanding of caste, and self-righteous tendencies in the Left that refuses to listen and learn that social change cannot be programmed, scientific and sanitised but carries with it a load of uncertainties that need to be incessantly made sense of and within them find the possibilities to break the condensation of the polity into a majoritarian construct. Majoritarianism in Indian polity today is growing in the interstices of secular sectarianism that left unanswered various inconvenient questions pertaining to social groups that were considered as the subaltern. It is within this space and growing possibility of conflicts within the subaltern on the one hand, and joining in alliance with the traditional social elite on the other that rightwing political mobilisation is finding its new space and turning democracy on its head.

Published in *The Hindu*, November 20, 2014.

45

Is There a Future for the Congress?

Rahul Gandhi has performed a series of cameo roles and failed to make the big impact Congress is looking for. He is searching for an image that will propel him into an acceptable and legitimate leader of a national party with a long legacy in India. All his predecessors have had the advantage of catapulting themselves into national leaders riding on a wave, Rajiv Gandhi after the assassination of Indira Gandhi and Sonia after the death of Rajiv Gandhi. Rahul has had no such wave but has had instead the arduous task of inventing an image that can in fact create a wave in his favour and it is, perhaps, the changing nature of Indian democracy that has eluded him such favourable context. Over the last few years, Rahul Gandhi made a series of experiments of constructing an image for himself. If we pause and interrogate he was in the news for a range of consciously and cautiously conducted experiments including his breach of security for travelling in sleeper class to Gorakhpur to enquire about the plight of the migrants, as he did earlier by travelling in the local in Mumbai; he conveyed the desire of the student organisations in UP to have elections for student bodies to the Ministry of Human Resources; before that he was busy campaigning for development and the rural poor in Bihar, 'compelling' his fellow Congressmen to commit the blasphemy of comparing him to Jayaprakash Narayan which was only putting in a metaphorical language Rahul's carefully crafted persona of a social activist. He did not hesitate, on an earlier occasion, to even go public with regard to the issue of displacement of the tribals of Niyamgiri hills in Orissa, when he assured them that he was their 'foot-soldier' and will carry forward their battles right up to the power-centres in Delhi.

The image of a social activist, a rebel or a messiah of the downtrodden raised the obvious question as to who is Rahul Gandhi fighting against and whose government is in power in any case? Why does he need to take a posturing against his own government? This seems to be the sordid story of achieving growth with the rhetoric of equity. The formidable combination of Manmohan-Montek is only too happy to carry forward the growth story with repeated public statements on achieving 8% growth rate and suggested target of crossing into double figures by next year, creating an investment-friendly climate for global capital flows and incentives to the corporate sector. The Prime Minister did not even hesitate to disallow free distribution of rotting rice to the poor, since it will, he claimed, damage the incentives to the farmers. These unabashed pronouncements are then, often, countered by Sonia and of late, Rahul Gandhi who have come across as those representing the equity part of the story. They are the 'dissenting' voices that raise the issues of adequate compensation for any land acquired for purposes of development, fight for implementation of the RTI; are in favour of the tribals and all those dispossessed by the current developmental path adopted by the Congress.

The current phase of economic reforms seems to be accompanied by a welfare dimension, without a welfare state. There is no visible long-term welfare policy structure in place, for instance either with regard to labour laws or social costs of production. However, there are any number of welfare policies in all the states governed by the Congress, ranging from the MGNREGS, to Indira Vikas Ayogan, subsidies to farmers, loan waivers, free electricity, Rs. 2 a kg rice schemes, free housing, to mention a few. The number of policies named after the Gandhi family was so wide-ranging that the various ministries had to be reminded that they need to use the 'brand' name of the Gandhi family with prudence. This, rather new mode of 'managing' growth with a discourse of equity, has led to new institutional arrangements. While the state institutions such as the Planning Commission are headed by neo-monetarists, the discourse of welfare seems to have more space outside the state either through the political parties, individual leaders or to be found in semi-governmental bodies such as the NAC with social activists, such as Jean Dreze and Aruna Roy who have been championing causes that include rehauling of the PDS. This allows the state on the one hand to continue with a long-term undivided focus on growth-oriented policies, and the Gandhi family to retain their welfare, if not a socialist rhetoric. This new institutional arrangement has led to a new culture of dissenters being tolerated within the Congress. While the likes of Digvijay Singh make noises on all sorts of issues, including adverse comments on their allies to rein them in, others like Mani Shankar Aiyar have stayed in the headlines with his anti-CWG statements to the extent of saying that he would have been happy if the games did not take place. It is important to observe that this range and intensity of dissent is allowed only for all those outside the government, and not for either those in the government holding various ministries or even those such as the former media adviser to the PMO who was chastised for going public in critiquing the Congress as a status-quoist party. In fact, the Prime Minister had to finally claim that his cabinet is more cohesive than even Nehru's. The dissenting voices are being tolerated, as never before, in the history of the Congress. This could well be a carefully crafted strategy of the Congress but it has not, at least for Rahul Gandhi, worked favourably. After his party's debacle in UP and Bihar, it is obvious that Rahul needs a new image make-over but what is a convincing image that can make him a legitimate and credible leader is the most challenging of questions, and how this is going to play out will hold some important clues as to what is to happen to dynasty rule in a democracy. It is not Modi which is the biggest challenge, as much of media reports and political rhetoric has made it out to be but this failure in finding an acceptable image among the electorate that continues to hurt the interests and prospects of Congress in the coming elections.

Published in *Hans India*, March 22, 2013.

The Citizenship Debate

46

Reducing the Citizen to a Consumer

Review of Citizenship and Its Discontents—An Indian History *by Niraja Gopal Jayal (Permanent Black, Delhi, 2014).*

This book, among other issues, raises two very pertinent questions regarding the constitutional and democratic processes in post-independence India. Firstly, "unlike in the West, where differentiated citizenship rights emerged in consolidated civic communities, the Indian recognition of rights accruing to collectivities rather than individuals occurred in a society which lacked the prior foundations of a civic community. It is not clear as to whether and to what extent community-mediated rights are compatible with a civic community if they precede the construction of the latter". Secondly, it asks, "the paradox is that social citizenship was at its weakest when the socialist rhetoric was at its peak, and has gained momentum in a policy environment that emphasises state withdrawal from public provisioning. How and why these rights have emerged on the Indian political landscape in a time of ascendant neoliberalism, and increasing commodification of public services...".

The question of the emergent tension between ascriptive community identities and civic community, and the paradox of expansion of welfare during the rise of neoliberal economic order are at the heart of understanding the story of what has happened to constitutional values and the project of social citizenship in India. However, the book would have made a more complex case had it looked at the interface of all three processes together, between identity politics, civic community and neoliberal economic order.

The story of contemporary Indian politics is precisely the tension between these three dimensions. While identity politics has enormously helped in mobilising and giving voice to some of the most marginalised communities, yet it degenerated into entrenched sectarianism and perpetuated conflicts between the subaltern using the language of rights against each other, the idea of civic foundation while it promoted a degree of constitutional values in public life and some dynamism into institutions, it is increasingly taking the ugly turn of majoritarianism in the name of Hindu nationalism; and finally, neoliberal order while ushering in growth has, willy-nilly helped in expanding the social welfare frame, while hitting hard at the very foundations of civic solidarity and further dispossessing the marginalised groups that had marshalled culture and identity to regain space within the political community.

The question that really should concern us is whether or not the dynamism and the tension between these dimensions are proving to be productive for a democratic project in India. Or, on the contrary, is the assumed open-endedness of these processes converting into a new hegemonic order through a certain kind of a new combination between these processes?

The book under review takes a more predictable and well-known trajectory of the immense possibility of expansion of social citizenship through institutionalised Constitutional and institutional dynamics. I would argue, somewhat in contrast, that the breakdown of civic foundations is re-emerging through a stronger call of nationalism, patriotism and Hindu nationalism, which is actively aided, not contested, by the turn identity politics and the language of differentiated citizenship has taken over the last two decades. The massive fragmentation of identities, intra-subaltern conflicts, and the use of rights language and its given competitive frame is making the majoritarian turn of the civic foundation increasingly attractive to the subaltern who hitherto spoke the language of differentiation and heterogeneity.

The subaltern now perceives her interests in the dominant project, while at the other extreme end of the political spectrum, they have taken to militant politics that Jayal refers to in her chapter on backwardness. The subaltern is caught between powerlessness and militancy. It is in this context that neoliberalism adds its own distinct version of market fundamentalism to overbearing majoritarian religious fundamentalism.

The story is one of indomitable convergence between these two kinds of fundamentalism that is specific to how one could approach the important questions that Jayal raises in her book. Neoliberal order is simultaneously allowing for cultural assertion and economic dispossession. This in turn often propels essentialism of cultural identities. What is being disallowed in economic terms is made good through a sense of cultural empowerment and cultural exclusion.

Citizenship has always been as much a process of exclusion as it remains a means for inclusion. Citizenship in liberal discourse draws more from the contractual tradition imbricated in quid pro quo action rather than substantive solidarity. Social contract is, simply put, the social version of contractualism — exchange relations — of the market. It is therefore not a surprise that the citizen-subject is seamlessly merging into the consumer-subject. In fact, citizenship today makes sense more in terms of consumption patterns and service-delivery rather than the language of equality and fraternity.

The story only becomes more complex when one finds epistemic roots of the rights discourse too in the competitive logic of the market. What therefore is the missing link is 'class abatement' of the citizenship project as T.H. Marshall had argued in the 1950s. Instead, we have witnessed the expansion of the governmental mechanisms at the cost of participatory ethos, reducing participation to what Partha Chatterjee refers to as 'contextual negotiation', as the only survival strategy viable for the subaltern; though Chatterjee speaks in an affirmative tone of finding subaltern agency in these microscopic activities of the subaltern.

It is therefore understandable, as Jayal rightly points out that, "it is deeply ironical that the moment of active citizenship coincides with a denial of the legitimacy of politics". While the political itself remains extremely constrained, we are witnessing attempts to replace or subsume it under a new moral and social language of the civil society over not so civil or civic conditions of our everyday reality.

Published in *The Hindu*, July 1, 2014.

47

Explaining Democracy in India

Lloyd I. Rudolph and Susanne Hoeber Rudolph, *Explaining Indian Democracy: A Fifty Year Perspective, 1956–2006*, New Delhi, Oxford University Press, 2008.

Vol. I: *The Realm of Ideas: Inquiry and Theory*

Vol. II: *The Realm of Institutions: State Formation and Institutional Change*

Vol. III: *The Realm of the Public Sphere: Identity and Policy*.

Susanne Rudolph and Lloyd Rudolph have been leading political scientists researching and writing together, on a range of issues concerning India and its democracy, for well over four decades now. The three volumes under review bring together most of their published articles in various journals and edited volumes, apart from select chapters from their books. Writing from an 'area studies' perspective that privileges 'situated knowledge, knowledge that is located and marked by time and place and circumstance', they not only prodded American political scientists to look beyond formal modelling and rational choice but also offered completely fresh insights on almost all the problems that have attracted their attention. Some of these formulations, whether one agrees with them or not, continue to be central to our understanding and framing of issues of democracy in India.

Volume I titled *Realm of Ideas: Inquiry and Theory* brings together some of their finest essays on methodology and epistemology including an essay that privileges subjective knowledge located in personal experience and cultural tradition, as against objective knowledge 'that is knowledge based on a view from nowhere; unmediated, transparent observation generated by unmarked and unencumbered observers' (p. 75). Similarly, the essay on 'imperialism of categories' questions American scholars who stand steadfast on a 'liberal absolutism indifferent to difference', while the article on consensus and conflict in Indian politics attributes the privileging of consensus unique to the way politics are framed in India to 'the romance and reality that surrounds the image of the village in Indian mind' (p. 144). In the following section they explore their classic formulation on 'modernity of tradition' that 'accords tradition a higher priority in the study of modernisation' (p. 164), and even insist on this approach to clarify the myths about modern institutions and modernity as such. This central concern is carried over to their essay on bureaucracy where the Rudolphs reject Weber's ideal-type distinctions, and make a case that in most societies 'patrimonial, bureaucratic and charismatic features are more akin to a field of force that, depending on circumstances, variably conditions administrative behaviour and effectiveness' (p. 198); in the excerpt from the other classic book of theirs, *The Pursuit of Lakshmi*, they explore the reasons for the 'marginality of class politics' due to the state emerging as the third actor mediating the relations between capital and labour; reflecting on the role of media they explain how a serial such as *Ramayana* though projected tolerant ethos contextually becomes part of a conjunction for the demand to build a Ram temple in Ayodhya; tackling the tangled issue of uniform civil code they are optimistic of the possibility of achieving a balance in liberal democracies between protecting minority identity and 'yet moving towards greater uniformity of rights'.

Volume II is titled *The Realm of Institutions: State Formation and Institutional Change*. The first section has essays dealing with state formation in India along with comparative essays on Asia, wherein they primarily distinguish the processes of state formation from Europe on the basis of these entering into accommodation with feudalism rather than obliterating it—a position close to Kosambi's classical formulation on mode of production changing 'through adjustment and not displacement' (though he does not find a mention in their references); they also map the changes in the modern state that has become contested through the growing erosion of monopoly sovereignty with the opening of 'transnational spaces'. As part of understanding the process of institutional change in India, they take a look at all the possible significant issues concerning state institutions beginning with the civil–military relation, and enquire as to why 'military services have played a limited role while in neighbouring Pakistan the story is very different' (this could be of particular interest to the readers given the current developments in Pakistan); they also include essays on judicial versus parliamentary sovereignty, and the (in)famous textbook controversy; further, their essays give a sense of the changing trajectory of democracy through the shift in focus from the contestation between 'demand polity' and 'command polity', marking the conflict of interests between 'ascendancy of voter sovereignty' as against the 'ascendancy of state sovereignty' to the emergence of federal market economy that has inaugurated the process of delinking the state's economic fates from one another and fostering ' provincial Darwinism', coupled with the shift of the centre from an interventionist to a regulatory state.

Volume III is titled *The Realm of the Public Sphere: Identity and Policy*, negotiating significant developments such as the increasing role of caste associations in what Rajini Kothari referred to as the 'secularisation of caste' by linking the 'mass electorate to the new democratic political processes'; it then examines the tricky question that the New Left theoreticians such as Herbert Marcuse were engaged with as to under what conditions do students convert themselves into a political class; the next section exclusively focuses on the foreign policy of the United States and its implications for achieving regional stability and the Rudolphs make the proposition that it is 'in the interest of the US to encourage equitable growth in South Asia' (p. 240); and, along the lines of what Richard Falk once famously called the 'terrorist foundations of US foreign policy', the volume cautions against the 'illusions of imperial nostalgia and strategic fantasy' reflected in the influence of Francis Fukuyama on policy formulations. The Rudolphs respond to Huntington's 'Clash of Civilisations' thesis, again along the lines of what Edward Said had termed as the 'Clash of Ignorance', by reiterating the 'bare fact' that 'religions are themselves internally contested—Vatican Catholocism and liberationism; modernist and fundamentalist Islam, nationalist and supranational arenas of faith' (p. 307). The last section turns to their interventions as 'public intellectuals' in various popular magazines and news dailies, on issues such as cows and election campaigns and the role of film stars in southern India, to finally conclude by explaining why India continues to survive as an 'organised chaos'.

This body of work would be essential in re-imagining the way political studies has been pursued in India, both by way of what they have focused on and what they have missed out and preferred to ignore. Theirs has been a journey that was interested in studying societies as a whole that was 'problem-driven' in contrast to the growing number of political scientists who choose to settle down with ever-narrower areas or subject-matter of study with blinkers that incapacitate them to look no further however strong the imperatives of an 'integrated material life' and the overflowing 'surplus' that belies the self-imposed enclosures. The thematic focus of the studies by the Rudolphs caution us against needless and compelling dovetailing into safe havens of being bound within the limits of political theory or 'Indian Politics' or 'International Relations'. They moved from political economy to culture, to comparative methods, and the historical method based on primary sources (their essay on Amar Singh's diaries, published in the *Indian Economic and Social History Review*), and they 'deplored the deep and enduring split between theory and empirical research in political science' (p. 139). Life and 'experience', as E.P. Thompson once eloquently put it, 'does not wait discreetly outside their (read philosophers) offices, waiting for a moment at which the discourse of proof will summon in into attendance. Experience walks in without knocking at the door...' Both 'theoretical imperialism' and the massive confusion between empiricism (including source fetishism of some disciplines) and the 'empirical mode of intellectual practice' have pushed political scientists to draw artificial self-referential boundaries and give up the study of societies in their manifold interconnections for 'specialised' and 'regionally enclosed' studies.

Finally, in spite of the vastness of the areas and issues they have studied, or precisely for this reason, one is struck by the limitation of restricting themselves to the 'high-politics' of politics in the 'mainland', especially in understanding the nature of democracy in India. They have completely neglected in 'explaining Indian democracy' the plight of the peripheries beginning with the 'colonial hinterlands' in the north-eastern parts of India, to the war-ravaged Kashmir. Attempting to explain the growing practice of extra-judicial killings of not just militants but unarmed civilians (including religious minorities) and its justification by all organs of the government, civil war-like conditions in many parts of India would have dramatically changed the way they have approached and formulated some of their ideas such as around centrism. While, for instance, centrism remains a challenge for all political articulations, helping us to explain many of the phenomenon including the recent shift in the Bahujan Samaj Party (BSP) from Bahujan to Sarvajan, it nevertheless would have completely different implications for some of the social groups and spaces reconfiguring our idea of not only centrist politics but the nature of democracy itself in India. This also takes us to their more recent flirting with post-modernism, in their book titled the *Postmodern Gandhi*, and provides an occasion to revisit the question as to what could be the possible meeting ground between liberalism and post-modernism, apart from their reference to Mill's emphasis on 'tentative truths' and Gandhi's reiteration, according to them, of 'contingent and contextual truth'. Do then liberalism and certain variants of post-colonial arguments that share much in common with the post in post-modernism also have certain underlying convergence?

The sheer depth and breadth of issues covered in these three volumes make them an indispensable read, to not just students of political science but all those interested in the understanding of what has been happening, and not happening, with democracy in India.

Published in the *Indian Economic & Social History Review* (IESHR).